THE GREAT CIRCLE

A HISTORY OF THE FIRST NATIONS

NEIL PHILIP

Foreword by Dennis Hastings

CLARION BOOKS
NEW YORK

Mitakuye oyasin—
All my relatives

Clarion Books
a Houghton Mifflin Company imprint
215 Park Avenue South, New York, NY 10003
Copyright © 2006 by Neil Philip
Foreword © 2006 by Dennis Hastings
Published in the United States in 2006 by arrangement with
The Albion Press Ltd, Spring Hill, Idbury, Oxfordshire OX7 6RU, England

Designed by Emma Bradford.
The text was set in 13-point Garamond Book.
Map by Kayley LeFaiver

For information about permission to reproduce selections from this book, write to
Permissions, Houghton Mifflin Company, 215 Park Avenue South, New York, NY 10003.

www.houghtonmifflinbooks.com

Library of Congress Cataloging-in-Publication Data

Philip, Neil.
    The great circle : a history of the First Nations / Neil Philip ;
foreword by Dennis Hastings.
        p. cm.
    Includes bibliographical references and index.
    ISBN-13: 978-0-618-15941-3
    ISBN-10: 0-618-15941-X
    1. Indians of North America—History. 2. Indians of North
America—Government relations. 3. Indians of North America—Social
life and customs. I. Title.
    E77.P48 2006
    973.04′97—dc22

                                                    2005032743

10 9 8 7 6 5 4 3 2 1

Typesetting: Servis Filmsetting Ltd, Manchester
Printed in China by South China Printing Co.

ENDPAPERS: Joseph Kossuth Dixon *Climbing the western slope* 1913
TITLE PAGE: Edward Sheriff Curtis *Hopi pottery drying* 1922
CONTENTS PAGE: *Apache medicine sash* 19th century
OPPOSITE FOREWORD: Edward Sheriff Curtis *Comanche girl* 1930

CONTENTS

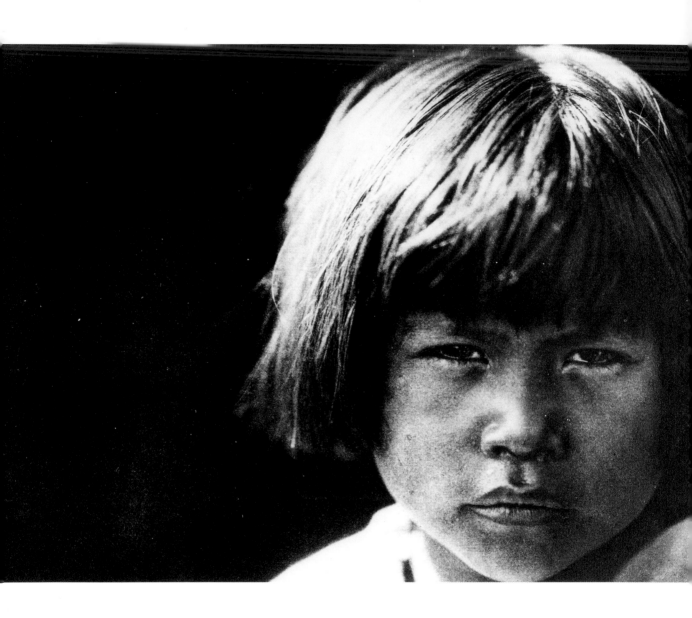

FOREWORD

I am happy to introduce *The Great Circle: A History of the First Nations*. For too long, Indian history has been distorted, ignored, and marginalized. *The Great Circle* is a step in setting the record straight. Speaking for the Umoⁿhoⁿ (Omaha) Tribe of Nebraska and Iowa, of which I am a member, I can attest to its accuracy concerning the proud history of the Umoⁿhoⁿ, which reaches back to the mound builders of Ohio, and forward through many changes to the present day. I am grateful to Neil Philip for making the effort (as many past writers have not) to contact us to verify the information in his manuscript.

If we are to begin to understand the Indian Nations, books like *The Great Circle* are badly needed by our reservations schools as well as by the general public. Especially in a country like the United States, where people of many nationalities have settled among the First Nations, it is particularly important for every group to be able to tell its own history. Only when we are willing to listen to all of these stories will we reach a full understanding of who we are, and what path we came down. Only with this vital knowledge can we hope to build a solid future that includes everyone.

Dennis Hastings, M.A.
Director, Omaha Tribal Historical Research Project, Inc.

INTRODUCTION

This is a book about the history of the First Nations who have lived in North America at least since the last Ice Age. No book could include all the individuals and events that make up that history; I have had to select a handful of topics to cover in detail. These include some of the most dramatic moments in the story of the Native Americans—first contact with European invaders, Tecumseh's attempt to unite the First Nations, Chief Joseph's doomed but valiant war in defense of his people's land, the brutal massacre of unarmed Cheyennes at Sand Creek—chosen to best reflect the broad sweep of the Indian experience. Many nations are not even mentioned in the text, but their griefs and hopes are woven into the wider pattern that underlies each individual story.

The book takes its title from words spoken by the Lakota holy man Black Elk (Hehaka Sapa). "The power of the world always works in circles," he said, "and everything tries to be round."

These words seem to me to sum up the tragedy of Indian-white relations. The Indians thought of the world as a great sacred circle; the whites thought of it as a straight line like a railway track, gathering pace on the journey "from savagery, through barbarism and civilization, up to enlightenment." This view of progress is quoted from the *23rd Annual Report of the Bureau of American Ethnology, 1901-2*; it was written by the Bureau's director, J. W. Powell.

This philosophy would have been shared by most whites at the time, and is still the basis of the western worldview. But it would have made no sense whatsoever to Black Elk.

Edward Sheriff Curtis
Navajo smile 1904

One of the most important Navajo deities is Changing Woman, the creator of the Navajo people, whose name reflects her nature. In winter she is a bent old woman, but she gradually regains her youth, until she becomes "a young girl so beautiful that we bowed our heads in wonder." This endless cycle of renewal is another example of the way Native American thought interprets the world as a sacred circle.

Edward Sheriff Curtis
The Vanishing Race
1904

*E. S. Curtis chose this
picture as the first plate
in his monumental
20-volume work* The
North American Indian,
*published between 1907
and 1930. He wrote,
"The thought which this
picture is meant to
convey is that the
Indians as a race,
already shorn of their
tribal strength and
stripped of their
primitive dress, are
passing into the
darkness of an
unknown future."
The Navajo have always
viewed the world as a
highly dangerous place,
but it is unlikely that
the Navajos in this
photograph thought of
themselves or their
culture as irretrievably
doomed; the mistaken
idea of the "Vanishing
Race" reflects a
romanticized white
perspective rather than
an Indian viewpoint.*

For him, enlightenment meant understanding Creation, not controlling it.

It would be easy to write a history of the Native Americans that was simply a long list of atrocities. Indeed, their story is blighted by terrible tragedy and injustice. In this book I hope to show how that history was shaped by the clash of worldviews between the Indians and the whites—most obviously in the two conflicting ideas about the ownership of the land. For the Indians, the idea of buying and selling land was as silly as the notion of buying and selling one's soul. But land ownership was the very basis of the white man's economy.

In telling the story of the Native Americans since Columbus, I have tried to balance the views of the Indians and the whites. I have placed reliance on the written testimony of whites but have given equal weight to the oral traditions of Indians.

On the facing page is a famous photograph by Edward S. Curtis, who devoted his life to recording in words and photographs the world of the Native Americans. It is a study of a group of Navajo (Diné) taken in 1904. They are on horseback, and the photograph shows them melting into the twilight. Curtis titled the work "The Vanishing Race."

This assumption that by the early twentieth century the Native Americans were on the point of cultural extinction was shared by many, and for good reason. The previous century had seen the proud and thriving nation of the Mandan reduced to a pitiful remnant by the ravages of smallpox, the Cherokee driven from their land to follow the bitter Trail of Tears, the resistance of the Lakota finally crushed at the massacre of Wounded Knee.

Yet the Navajo, far from vanishing, have flourished. They are now probably more numerous than at any time in their history. In 1868, when they endured the Long Walk to their new reservation from captivity in Fort Sumner, New

Mexico, the Navajo numbered around 10,000. Today there are around 250,000 Navajo. The Navajo Nation has its own tribal council, its own office in Washington D.C. to lobby politicians on its behalf, and a thriving community college; the Navajo are enmeshed in the fabric of modern American life. They can boast a world-famous poet, Luci Tapahonso; a world-famous golfer, Notah Begay; and a world-famous artist, Conrad House, who died prematurely in 2001. The language has survived, the culture has survived, the people have survived. They have not vanished.

The oldest inhabited settlement in North America is the Hopi pueblo of Oraibi in northeastern Arizona. The Hopi have lived there since around A.D. 1100, when they received a great revelation from Maasaw, the Guardian of the Earth. Today this vision of harmony still guides the life

George Ben Wittick
Hopi girls of Oraibi
1898

These Hopi girls were photographed inside the home of one of them, Masha-Honka-Shi. Their elaborate "side-whorl" hairstyles identify them as unmarried. The years following the taking of this photograph were to bitterly divide the Hopis of Oraibi between progressive "Friendlies" and traditionalist "Hostiles." On September 7, 1906, the two groups held a traditional pushing contest to decide supremacy; the traditionalists lost, and were expelled from Oraibi. They founded a new village at Hotevilla, taking with them the sacred Pathway stone tablet, on which the Hopi prophecies are engraved. They also buried at Hotevilla a sacred object that is regarded as the source of the spiritual power needed to keep the universe in balance.

and thought of the nation whose name means "The People of Peace." Put simply, traditionalist Hopis believe that by following their "Hopi Way," they maintain the balance of the whole world. Hopi mythology tells us that this world in which we live is the fourth in a series of seven worlds, and foretells that in the near future it will come to an end and the fifth world will be born.

A Hopi named Don Monongye testified to the depth and sincerity of this belief when speaking in the 1955 Hopi hearings held by the Bureau of Indian Affairs. He quoted his father's words: "I am from the Sand clan whose duty it is to keep this earth and life going." Whether one accepts this mission as true, either literally or symbolically, or dismisses it as unreal, it is still an expression of the human spirit at its noblest.

Throughout his long life, the Lakota holy man Black Elk was guided by the great vision that came to him when he was nine years old. Taken to a mountaintop at the center of the world, he looked down on "the whole hoop of the world."

> And I saw that the sacred hoop of my people was one of many hoops that made one circle, wide as daylight and as starlight, and in the center grew one mighty flowering tree to shelter all the children of one mother and one father. And I saw that it was holy.

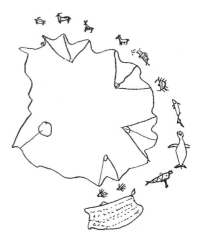

Santo Blanco
Map of Tiburon Island 1930

Tiburon, a rocky island in the Gulf of California, is the home of the Seri Nation. This drawing recalls how the god Ahnt ah koh'mah came from across the sea and taught the Seri how to make fire. He went round the island, showing how to kill the animals that lived there, and how to cook and eat them. Then he made trails from the beach to the waterholes.

A NOTE ON TERMINOLOGY

Anyone writing on Native American topics enters a minefield of conflicting names and terms. No overall term for the indigenous peoples of North America is generally accepted—"Native Americans" or just "Natives" is as offensive to some as "Indians" is to others. In Canada "First Nations" is commonly used. In this book I use all of these terms, depending on the context, and vary the usage to prevent undue repetition.

In a general history like this, such catchall terms cannot be avoided. But as the details of the book will make clear, the Native North Americans are not a single homogenous people. The cultures of the First Nations—their languages, their traditions, their ways of life—are startlingly diverse. There are, however, also strong similarities among them, especially in their understanding of the spiritual power that infuses the whole of the natural world. There are tragic similarities, too, in the challenges and disasters that faced each nation in turn as it encountered the whites.

For individual nations I have tried to use names and spellings currently accepted by those nations themselves (for instance, on official websites). Thus I refer to the Nuxalk Nation rather than the Bella Coola Indians, but to the Cherokee and not the Tsalagi or the Aniyunwiya. Alternative names are often given in parentheses. The most complicated case is that of the nation still commonly known as the Sioux. This name (a French adaptation of the name given them by an enemy tribe, the Ojibwe) is now deemed offensive, but there is no comparable term that includes all three divisions of the Sioux Nation: the Lakota (Teton), Dakota (Santee), and Nakota (Yankton). These groups speak distinct but mutually intelligible dialects of the same language and share a common history and culture. Because Lakota chiefs such as Red Cloud, Sitting Bull, and Crazy Horse figure so prominently in this history, I use the term Lakota to mean the Sioux as a whole, and specify Santee, Yankton, or Teton—or one of the seven Teton tribes such as the Sichangu (Brule), Oglala, Hunkpapa, or Mnikowoju—where this is necessary.

Where I refer to a people in the singular—for instance, the Cherokee—it means the nation as a whole. Where I use the plural—the Cherokees—the context should make clear which particular group of individuals from that nation is intended.

Native American people often had several names in their own language (many spelled differently in every source book!) as well as names by which they were known to the whites. Again, I have tried where possible to use the most appropriate name, and to give alternatives. In some cases, the white name is so well known that it would be pedantic and counterproductive to use the Indian one. So I refer to Sitting Bull, not Tatanka Iyotanka, and to Captain Jack, not Kintpuash.

I hope it will be clear to every reader that, whatever names or terms I use, no offense or disrespect is intended to any individual or group.

As to geographical names, in most cases I have used current terms, many of which, of course, postdate the events described; this should be clear from the context.

To pronounce the Indian names, read them as they look, syllable by syllable.

Anon.
Native drawing of the Ghost Dance
c. 1892

A Comanche drawing of the Ghost Dance, collected by the ethnologist James Mooney. The Ghost Dance religion of 1890 prophesied the coming renewal of the world, in which the Indians would regain all they had lost and the whites would be swept away. The dancers entered a kind of trance in which they visited the spirit world.

Culture Groups and Tribes

Groups are indicated on the map by letters,
and tribes are indicated by numbers.

A. Arctic
  1. Inuit

B. Californian
  2. Yana

C. Great Basin
  3. Northern Paiute

D. Northeastern
  4. Mashantucket Pequot
  5. Seneca
  6. Shawnee
  7. North Carolina Algonquians

E. Northwest Coast
  8. Nuu-chah-nulth (Nootka)
  9. Nuxalk (Bella Coola)

F. Plains
  10. Lakota (Sioux or Teton)
  11. Santee (Dakota)
  12. Omaha

G. Plateau
  13. Modoc
  14. Nez Perce

H. Southeastern
  15. Cherokee
  16. Seminole

I. Southwestern
  17. Akimel O'odham (Pima)
  18. Apache
  19. Navajo

J. Subarctic
  20. Tli Cho (Dogrib)

International boundaries
State/province boundaries
Culture group boundaries

N
W   E
S

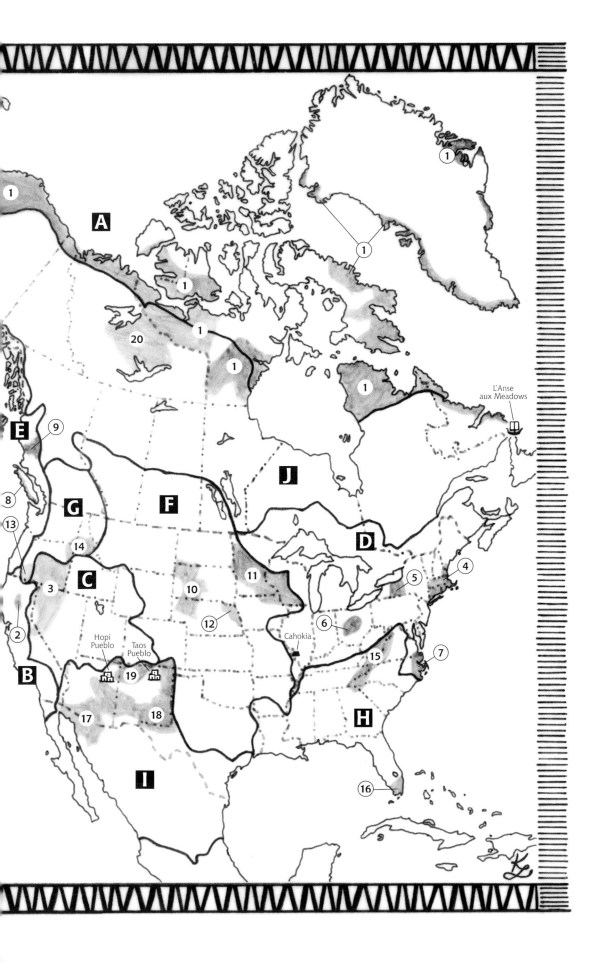

L'Anse
aux Meadows

Hopi
Pueblo

Taos
Pueblo

Cahokia

A

E

9

8

13

G

14

C

3

2

B

19

17

18

I

F

J

D

11

10

12

4

5

6

15

7

H

16

1

1

1

1

1

1

20

Their rype corne.

Their greene corne.

Corne newly sprong.

Their sitting at meate.

The place of solemne prayer.

The house wherin the Tombe of their Herounds standeth.

SECOTON

A Ceremony in their prayers wth strange testurs and songs dansing abowt posts carued on the topps lyke mens faces.

1 THE EARTH IS OUR MOTHER

My children, when at first I liked the whites,
My children, when at first I liked the whites,
I gave them fruits,
I gave them fruits.

Arapaho (Inuna-ina) Ghost Dance song,
translated by James Mooney

A Cherokee myth tells how at the Creation a rock was given to the white man and a piece of silver to the Indian. Both threw the gifts away, thinking them of no value. Later, the white man picked up the silver, recognizing its value as currency, and has kept it in his pocket ever since. The Indian picked up the rock and, recognizing it as a storehouse of sacred power, has kept it ever since.

The differing value systems of the Europeans who settled North America after 1492—primarily the Spanish, French, Dutch, and English—and the Native inhabitants lie at the root of all the conflicts and misunderstandings that have blighted Indian-white relations from the beginning.

Most histories of North America begin with the "discovery" of the New World by Cristóbal Colón (or Christopher Columbus, as he is better known) in 1492. In fact, Columbus was not the first to sail to North America. Vikings under Leif Ericson reached what they called Vinland (the land of vines) some five hundred years earlier, around A.D. 1000. The site of a Viking settlement has been excavated at L'Anse aux Meadows in Newfoundland. So far as we know, only one Viking child was born in North America—Snorri, the son of Thorfinn Karlsefni (leader of

John White
The village of the Secotan 1585

The artist John White made six voyages to America, including the reconnaissance trip to Roanoke in 1584 and the settlement voyage the following year, during which he made a detailed visual record of the Carolina Algonquians. He returned as governor of the ill-fated second Roanoke colony in 1587, and went back to England later that year. His drawings were well observed and accurate. This one depicts the village of the Secotan as an open village of about ten wooden houses. It would have been home to between a hundred and two hundred people; other similar-sized villages, such as that of the Pomeioc, were enclosed by a circular palisade. The drawing shows how the Secotan planted their corn in sequence, to ensure three harvests. In the winter they left the village to live by hunting, fishing, and gathering wild crops.

Anon.
Mooring holes 1555

This engraving shows how the Vikings secured their ships to mooring rings anchored in rock. "Mooring holes" found in rocks in New England and Minnesota have been put forward as evidence of the Viking voyages, but most are probably side-products of quarrying. Although the Vinland voyages and the Viking settlement at L'Anse aux Meadows are indisputable facts, many of the Viking artifacts discovered in North America are hoaxes (like the famous Kensington rune stone), mementos of fur traders, or simple wishful thinking. For instance, the Newport Tower in Rhode Island, once believed to be a Viking monument, was almost certainly built around 1677 by the island's governor, Benedict Arnold.

the third expedition to Vinland) and Gudrid (his wife, the widow of Leif's brother Thorvald).

The Vikings called the native peoples they encountered in Vinland by the derogatory nickname "skraelings," which in Old Norse means something like "scared weaklings." No doubt the people of the First Nations were rightly wary of the large, well-armed, belligerent Vikings. When the second Viking party, led by Thorvald, saw three hide-covered boats on the beach, with three men asleep under each of them, they killed eight of the men. Later a skraeling emerged from the trees on the shoreline to shoot Thorvald Ericson in the stomach. Drawing the arrow from his gut, Thorvald said, "A fat paunch that was. We've found a land of fine resources, though we'll hardly enjoy much of them." Thorvald died soon after.

When Thorfinn Karlsefni led a third voyage, with sixty men and five women, the skraelings must have been on their guard. Yet initial contacts were friendly, and the two peoples soon began to trade with each other. Thorfinn was reluctant to trade away the swords and spears the skraeling wanted but happy to trade Norse red cloth for fur pelts.

In the second winter things turned ugly. This time when skraelings came to trade, one of them tried to take a weapon, and one of Thorfinn's servants killed him. The skraelings came back in force, and the first recorded battle between Europeans and Native Americans took place. According to the Greenlanders' Saga, "a large number of the natives were killed." The skraelings involved in this battle were probably ancestors of the M'ikmaq-Maliseet (Micmac).

The Viking dream of settling the New World failed because the Norsemen were greatly outnumbered by the Native inhabitants—and, having scornfully named them skraelings, had come to understand that they were neither scared nor weak. But this abortive European invasion set the pattern for much that was to follow. The dismissive attitude toward the indigenous people, the disregard for their land and hunting rights, the willingness to kill them on sight, the reluctance to trade fairly leading to disagreements and then brutal hostilities—all of these were to become all too familiar in Native American history.

When Columbus arrived in the Caribbean in 1492, there were probably about seven million people in North America, living in six hundred separate nations, speaking a great variety of languages, which scholars divide into sixty-two language families. Some of these language families, such as the Algonquian, are spread across the continent. Most of the nations first encountered by the whites on the eastern seaboard speak Algonquian languages, as do Plains peoples such as the Blackfoot, Cheyenne, and Arapaho; there are even two Californian languages, Wiyot and Yurok, that are linked to Algonquian. On the other hand, there are also languages, known as "isolates," spoken by only one people, such as the now-extinct Timucua language of Florida.

These Native nations had been living in their own clearly defined territories for at least ten thousand years, since the end of the last Ice Age. Modern science says that they came in several waves over a land bridge from Asia to Alaska, and then filtered down through the Americas. This scientific explanation is rejected by many Native Americans, as it runs counter to their sacred history. In Native American traditions, the Creator is usually said to have made the land for the people, and the people for the land.

George Meninock, a chief of the Yakama (Yakima) people, tried to explain this concept in his testimony during a 1915 trial for violating a Washington state code on salmon fishing.

> God created this Indian country and it was like he spread
> out a big blanket. He put the Indians on it. They were

created here in this country, truly and honestly, and that was the time this river started to run. . . . When we were created we were given our ground to live on, and from that time these were our rights. This is all true. . . . I was not brought from a foreign country and did not come here. I was put here by the Creator.

The intense reverence of Native Americans for the land—a belief expressed by the Nez Perce Dreamer priest Toohoolhoolzote in the words "The earth is part of my body"—made no sense to the white Europeans, who coveted their territory. Such statements, profoundly true for the Native Americans, seemed like superstitious nonsense to the whites, who had left their own homelands far away across the ocean. When Native American nations were removed from their land, they did not become homesick, they became truly sick. Many simply could not thrive away from the land where they belonged. The Apache warrior chief Geronimo (Goyathlay), in a plea from prison in Fort Sill, Oklahoma, wrote, "The Apaches and their homes [were] each created for the other by Usen [the Apache creator] himself. When they are taken from these homes, they sicken and die."

The First Nations had not been living an unchanging existence in an unspoiled paradise for ten thousand years. They fought one another, although in a limited way that produced minimal casualties, and the traditional histories of some nations record tribal migrations caused by war or famine.

There had been time, indeed, for great civilizations to rise and fall. In the southeast, a series of ever more sophisticated mound builder societies culminated in the Mississippian culture. The largest Mississippian city, now known as Cahokia (three miles from the Mississippi River in Illinois, across from St. Louis), lasted for seven hundred years, until a sudden and unexplained decline around A.D. 1150. Cahokia was a walled city of five square miles, home to more than ten thousand people, ruled by a monarch known as the Great Sun.

The peoples of the southeast such as the Natchez, Cherokee, Choctaw, and Chickasaw were the cultural inheritors of the Mississippians, while in the northeast the longhouse-dwelling nations of the Iroquois, as well as Plains nations such as the Omaha and Osage, were heirs to the Hopewell people who came before the Mississippians. In the southwest, the decline of the Anasazi led to the rise of the Pueblo nations, and the fall of the Hohokam gave birth to the Akimel O'odham and Tohono O'odham (the Pima and Papago). The Akimel O'odham in the Salt River Valley, Arizona, still use a system of canal irrigation devised by the Hohokam to make the desert bloom.

So North America had a rich and diverse cultural past in

Edward Sheriff Curtis
The sons of Chief Mnaínak 1911

Mnaínak, also known as George Meninock, was a chief of the Yakama, a Plateau people. In 1911, E. S. Curtis reckoned him "the man of greatest influence" among the Yakama. Historically, the Yakama were not a unified nation but rather a collection of loosely allied groups. It was not until 1855 (under their greatest leader, Kamiakin) that they formally joined together as the Confederated Tribes and Bands of the Yakima Nation.

1492, as well as a thriving present. But in important ways life before Columbus had stayed very much the same for centuries. The peoples of the First Nations were treading gently on Mother Earth, hunting and fishing and growing crops and skirmishing with their neighbors, unaware that everything they valued was about to be stripped from them.

Columbus claimed the New World for Spain and named its peoples *los indios,* the Indians. Within half a century the peaceful Arawak of the Caribbean islands had been wiped out by disease, massacre, and slavery.

By the time the first Spanish ship reached the mainland of North America in 1513, under the command of Juan Ponce de León, the Calusa of southern Florida had learned enough about the new menace on their doorstep to take to their war canoes and drive it off. Ponce de León returned with two hundred colonists in 1521, and was again repulsed. He himself was mortally wounded, but lived long enough to name the province Florida.

The Calusa were then a prosperous nation, with a great ceremonial center on the west coast island of Marco and many towns linked by a system of canals. Within two centuries of the European invasion, the Calusa Nation fragmented and disappeared, though some of its cultural heritage survived among the Seminole and Mikasuki.

The effect of incursions by Spanish conquistadors on Native American peoples was disastrous. The year 1540 found two Spanish expeditions cutting a trail of destruction and disease across the continent. Starting in 1539 Hernando de Soto, who had participated in Francisco Pizarro's brutal destruction of the Inca empire in Peru, led a hunt for gold across the southeast. Many of its peoples, such as the Timucua of northern Florida, were proud and strong, but they were totally unprepared for the onslaught of torture, slavery, and death that de Soto unleashed.

The chief of the Timucuan town of Acuera sent a defiant message when summoned to swear submission to the pope and the king of Spain.

> I am king in my land, and it is unnecessary for me to become the subject of a person who has no more vassals than I. I regard those men as vile and contemptible who subject themselves to the yoke of someone else when they can live as free men. Accordingly, I and all my people have vowed to die a hundred deaths to maintain the freedom of our land. This is our answer, both for the present and evermore.

This chief managed to drive de Soto from his territory, but many of the Timucua were induced to die a hundred deaths. The men of one town were roped together like cattle while the Spaniards cut them to pieces with swords. "It was very fortunate for our men that most of the Indians were in chains or other confinements," wrote a Spanish chronicler, "for they were valiant and spirited people, and had they found themselves free, would have done more harm."

De Soto's trail of death up the Mississippi reached its climax in a battle at Mabila, Alabama, with the Mobile Nation under Chief Tascalusa. Thousands of Mobiles died, but only about twenty of de Soto's men were killed, the Indian weapons and tactics generally causing injury rather than death. Only de Soto's own death from illness in 1542 brought the terror to an end; de Soto's demoralized men were driven back downriver by the Natchez, a nation that had inherited the cultural pride of the vanished Mississippians.

Worse was to come. Wherever they went, de Soto's men spread diseases to which the Native Americans had no resistance. When the Spaniards returned in 1559, the once-thriving kingdoms of the southeast had collapsed. They regrouped in years to come as the nations of the Creek Confederacy.

In the southwest the 1540 expedition of Francisco Vásquez de Coronado was initially less brutal. Lured by fairy tales of rich cities shining with gold and turquoise, Coronado was appalled to find only the mud-built pueblos. He had indeed discovered one of the world's great treasures, but cultural riches were not what he was looking for.

Failure to find the promised gold led to disappointment and frustration. When the Tiwa of Tiguex Pueblo rebelled after a Tiwa woman was assaulted by a Spaniard, Coronado smoked the people out of the kivas (the windowless chambers that are the sacred spaces of Pueblo religion), tied two hundred of them to stakes erected in the plaza, and burned them alive.

This was the start of a terrible era in Pueblo history. Their age-old religions repressed as superstition and devil

8

worship, the people of the pueblos were forcibly converted to Catholicism and ruled with fanatical cruelty. In the Pueblo Revolt of 1680, the Pueblos united under a San Juan medicine man named Popé and drove the Spaniards out. Twelve years later the Spaniards were back, but by then the power of Spain was already declining, and things were never so bad again.

In 1609 Dutch explorer Henry Hudson invited some Delaware chiefs onto his boat and plied them with brandy. In exchange for a few trinkets, he "bought" the island of Manhattan from his befuddled guests, who apart from anything else were simply a hunting party, with no particular claim to the land; the Delaware word Mannahattanik is said to mean "the place where we were all drunk." As this famous transaction shows, the European settlers did not take seriously the land rights of the indigenous inhabitants.

For instance, when the first English expedition landed in 1584, although they met with the chiefs of the Secotan Nation and traded with them, they simply claimed the land in the name of Queen Elizabeth I and called it Virginia, in honor of their Virgin Queen. A second expedition the next year built a fortified settlement on the island of Roanoke. Although welcomed with friendship by the Secotans, the English treated them with arrogance and also, like the Spaniards, unwittingly spread deadly diseases among them.

Pemisapan, the paramount chief of the Secotan Nation, decided to wage war, but his plans were betrayed to the English. The English struck first, Pemisapan was killed, and his people were slaughtered. Ten days later Sir Francis Drake arrived with his fleet and evacuated the half-starved English colony from Roanoke. A third expedition of 118 men, women, and children in 1587 had vanished without trace when its backer, Sir Walter Raleigh, returned in 1590 with supplies. A mestizo (mixed-race) people in North Carolina called the Lumbee claim descent from this lost colony.

De Lancey Gill
**William Terrill
Bradby** 1899

*William Terrill Bradby
was a chief of the
Pamunkey, a people
who were part of the
Powhatan confederacy.
Here he is dressed as
Wahunsenacawh, as
part of a re-enactment
of the story of John Smith
and Pocahontas.*

**The mantle
of Powhatan**
early 17th century

*This cloak is made from
the hides of seven white-
tailed deer, and is over
seven feet long. The
designs on the cloak are
made with shell beads;
the circles are believed
to represent the towns
of the Powhatan.
The human figure
may represent
Wahunsenacawh
himself, while the
animals may be spirit
helpers.*

At the beginning of the seventeenth century all the empire-building nations of Europe had toeholds in North America. The French built their first trading post at Port Royal in Nova Scotia in 1605; the Dutch claimed Manhattan in 1609; and in 1607 a new party of English colonists arrived in Chesapeake Bay and built Jamestown on the James River.

This site was in the territory of the chief Wahunsena-cawh, also known as Powhatan, the name of his nation. Wahunsenacawh ruled not only the Powhatan but thirty-one Algonquian nations who joined together as the Powhatan Confederacy. Alarmed at the fate of the Seco-tans, Wahunsenacawh had personal reason to be wary of white men, for his half brother Opechancanough, chief of the Pamunkey, had been captured in Chesapeake Bay by the Spanish in 1561 and baptized as Don Luis. He was unable to escape to his own people until 1570.

Nevertheless, Wahunsenacawh supplied the English fort with food and treated its people with respect. Many years later Captain John Smith related a romantic tale of how Wahunsenacawh's beautiful daughter Pocahontas saved him from her father's fury. This famous story is either pure fiction or a misunderstanding of the Native American custom by which women of the tribe may adopt captives to replace lost loved ones.

Smith was an arrogant and highhanded man, and disputes between the English and the Powhatan Confederacy led to war in 1609. The English were soundly beaten by Opechancanough's Pamunkey warriors. But the next year hundreds of new colonists arrived, and the tables were turned. In 1613 the English captured Pocahontas and offered to exchange her for all the English prisoners held by the Powhatan. Wahunsenacawh released the prisoners, but the English kept Pocahontas captive, baptizing her Lady Rebecca.

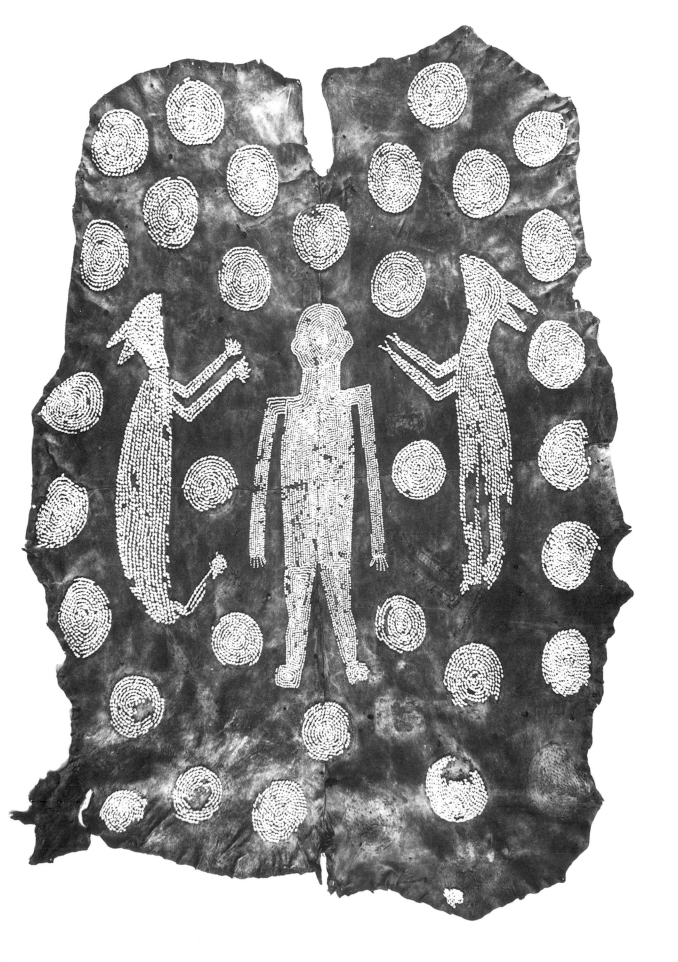

Thomas Vaughan
**Captain Smith
taking the King of
Pamunkey prisoner**
1624

*This engraving depicts a
1608 encounter between
Opechancanough and
Captain Smith, in which
the Englishman seized
Opechancanough by the
scalplock and threatened
him with a pistol. Smith
let Opechancanough go
free in exchange for a
regular tribute of corn,
necessary after a fire
had destroyed the
Jamestown colonists'
stores.*

In 1614 there was peace. Pocahontas married one of her captors, John Rolfe, and two years later sailed with him to England, where she and other Powhatans created a sensation at the royal court. In 1617 Pocahontas died of smallpox, aged just twenty-two; she is buried in a cemetery in Gravesend, England.

Wahunsenacawh's emissary Tomocomo returned home, bringing news not just of Pocahontas's death but of the enormous numbers of the English. It would be as easy, he said, to "count the stars in the sky, the leaves on the trees, or the sand upon the seashore" as to count the whites.

Wahunsenacawh abdicated his leadership, and as a result the Powhatan Confederacy fell apart.

His half brother Opechancanough remained hostile to the English, and with his medicine man, Nemattanew, at his side he waged a guerrilla war on the colonists. In 1623 the English invited him and hundreds of leading Indians to a peace conference, at which they served wine to toast "eternal friendship." The wine was poisoned, and many of the Indians died. But Opechancanough survived and continued to harry the English until 1644, when he was captured during one last attack. He was in his nineties, almost blind, crippled, and unable to walk; he had to be carried into battle. He was exhibited as a captive, and then one of his English guards shot him in the back.

The Mayflower Pilgrims founded the Plymouth Colony in 1620. The story of the colony's early years is one of the most peaceful accounts of white settlement. But the peacefulness is illusory. There was no immediate conflict because all Indians who had lived in the area around the colony had died from epidemics of European diseases. None had survived to dispute the Pilgrims' right to the land.

The Pilgrims were amazed when the first Indian they met, an Abenaki named Samoset, addressed them in the English language. "Welcome, Englishmen," he said. The story of how Massasoit, the chief of the Wampanoag Nation, made a peace treaty with the colonists, and celebrated with them the first Thanksgiving, is rightly one of the founding legends of America. The three-day celebration of friendship, harmony, and thankfulness for the gifts of Mother Earth might have signified a new and fruitful relationship between Natives and settlers.

But it was not to be. Massasoit's peace lasted for forty years, until his death. His sons Wamsutta and Metacom were less willing to compromise. The Wampanoag hunting lands were depleted, their traditions were suppressed, and

Anon.
Benjamin Church
Unknown date

Benjamin Church (1639-1717/8) was born at Plymouth, Massachusetts, and began life as a carpenter. He was commissioned a captain during King Philip's War (1675-76). His use of Indian troops and Indian tactics of warfare was innovative and successful. It was Church who captured Metacom's wife and son, who were then sold into slavery. After Metacom's death, Church ordered his body to be mutilated and denied burial; Metacom's head was exposed on a gibbet in Plymouth for the next twenty years.

the Christian religion was being forced upon them. After Wamsutta died, almost certainly poisoned while in English custody, Metacom began to speak out in defense of his people's religion, traditions, and rights.

> Brothers, you see this vast country before us, which the Creator gave to our fathers and us; you see the buffalo and deer that now are our support. Brothers, you see these little ones, our wives and children, who are looking to us for food and raiment; and you now see the foe before you, that they have grown insolent and bold; that all our ancient customs are disregarded; that treaties made by our fathers and us are broken, and all of us insulted; our council fires disregarded, and all the ancient customs of our fathers; our brothers murdered before our eyes, and their spirits cry to us for revenge. Brothers, these people from the unknown world will cut down our groves, spoil our hunting and planting grounds, and drive us and our children from the graves of our fathers, and our council fires, and enslave our women and children.

Such defiance could only lead to war. Metacom—better known to history under his English name, King Philip—rallied the Massachusetts Nations—the Nipmuck, Pocumtuck, Pocasset, Sokoki, and Hassanamesitt—to his cause and attacked the English settlements. Elsewhere along the coast other nations joined the fray.

The settlers responded vigorously, burning Indian villages and their inhabitants, and selling those who surrendered or were captured into slavery in Bermuda. When Metacom's wife, Wootonekanuske, and their infant son were sold as slaves, he said, "My heart breaks. Now I am ready to die."

Metacom was killed in 1676, and his alliance was crushed. Although six hundred English died in King Philip's War, more than three thousand Native Americans perished, and many of the nations of New England were almost wiped out.

The only confederacy of Indian nations to withstand the pressures of European settlers was the Iroquois League. This union of five Iroquoian peoples—the Seneca, Cayuga, Onondaga, Oneida, and Mohawk, with the addition of the Tuscarora after 1722—was well established before the Europeans arrived in North America. It originated with a vision by the prophet Deganawida, who saw a great spruce tree reaching up through the sky to the Master of Life. This was the Tree of the Great Peace, under which the Iroquoian peoples were to shelter, and beneath which they were to cast all their weapons of war: "We bury them from sight for ever, and plant again the Tree."

Although they were caught between the competing ambitions of the French and the English, the Iroquois managed to avoid major conflict with the whites. Until the Treaty of Paris in 1763, in which the French lost Canada and their lands east of the Mississippi to the English (and New Orleans and Louisiana west of the Mississippi to the Spanish), they remained relatively independent, partly because their lands south of Lake Ontario were strategically important for the fur trade.

Founding Fathers Benjamin Franklin and Thomas Jefferson studied and admired the Iroquois constitution as laid down by Deganawida, and Jefferson used it as a reference when framing the United States Constitution. There was indeed much to admire in this groundbreaking code, which established a true democracy, with equal rights for all individuals, both men and women, and which has lasted to this day. It provides for a legislature of fifty chiefs, called the Grand Council of the Haudenosaunee (the People of the Longhouse). Two of the places are never filled by living men, being reserved for the legendary founders of the League, Deganawida and Hiawatha. Deganawida's intention in creating this council was that "thinking will replace violence."

Onondaga wampum belt Unknown date

Wampum belts are made from strings of white or purple marine-shell beads; this example is forty-five rows wide and two hundred and forty rows long. They were often made to record and commemorate treaties and agreements, and also for use in rituals of kinship and condolence. The first wampum strings were said to have been made by Hiawatha, at the time that he and Deganawida founded the Iroquois League.

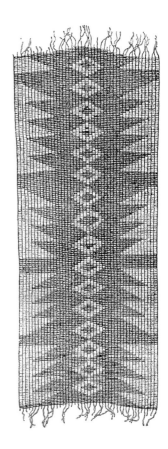

Historically, the Iroquois had closer links with the English than with the French, with whom they had been engaged in sporadic hostilities between 1653 and 1701. However, they chose not to take sides in the wars between France and England, preferring to use diplomacy to play one side against the other. After 1763, when the French ceded their territory to the English, the Iroquois lost the unique bargaining position they had achieved by balancing themselves between these rival European powers.

When the Ottawa Nation under Pontiac rose against the English in 1763, the Seneca joined in his attempt to drive the English settlers from Ohio, but most of the Iroquois held themselves neutral. In the American Revolution, the Grand Council again declared neutrality, but many Iroquois joined the British forces against the American colonists.

After the Revolution, the Iroquois rapidly lost much of their land in New York State. A Mohawk war chief, Joseph Brant, who had been a strong supporter of the British, negotiated some land in Canada in compensation, and as a consequence in 1784 the Iroquois League divided into two duplicate Grand Councils, one in Grande Rivière in Quebec and the other at Onondaga in New York.

The Iroquois have retained their political and cultural identity, thanks in part to a major revival of traditional religion. This renewal was begun in 1799 by the Seneca prophet Handsome Lake (Sganyadai:yo), the founder of the Longhouse religion that many Iroquois still follow.

Handsome Lake had a series of visions while seriously ill. In the first, three messengers from the Master of Life visited him, instructing him to give up alcohol, to root out witchcraft, and to ensure the continuance of the traditional Strawberry Festival. In his second vision, he was shown both heaven and hell and met Jesus, who showed him the nail holes in his hands and feet and complained bitterly that he had no true followers. In a third vision, the Master of Life warned him that the Haudenosaunee must keep up their traditional rituals, especially the Midwinter ceremony, or the world would be consumed by fire.

These visions effectively ordained Handsome Lake as the Iroquois messiah. Soon the People of the Longhouse were eagerly listening to his message. Although his moral teachings had a Christian tinge, his religion was also rooted in the deepest beliefs of the Iroquois. It provided them with the perfect framework in which to nurture and retain their traditional culture.

The Seneca chief Red Jacket (Sagoyewatha) showed in a speech of 1826 how completely Handsome Lake's teachings infused Iroquois thought.

after Charles Bird King
Red Jacket 1835–36

Red Jacket's English name apparently derives from the red coat he was given as a reward for services as a messenger for British officers during the American War of Independence. Red Jacket was a born diplomat and orator, who argued the cause of the Seneca with passion and logic. His chief opponents among the Seneca were those who had converted to Christianity, but he also clashed at times with the other leading Senecas of his day, such as Joseph Brant, Cornplanter, and Handsome Lake.

> There was a time when our forefathers owned this great island. Their seats extended from the rising to the setting sun. The Great Spirit had made it for use of Indians. He had created the buffalo, the deer, and other animals for food. He made the bear and the beaver, and their skins served us for clothing. He had scattered them over the country and taught us how to take them. He had caused the earth to produce corn for bread. All this he had done for his red children because he loved them. . . . But an evil day came upon us. Your forefathers crossed the great waters, and landed on this island. . . .
>
> Brother! Our seats were once large and yours were very small. You have now become a great people, and we have scarcely a place left to spread our blankets. You have got our country, but are not satisfied. You want to force your religion upon us. . . .
>
> Brother! The Great Spirit has made us all. But he has made a great difference between his white and red children. He has given us a different complexion and different customs. . . . Since he has made so great a difference between us in other things, why may we not conclude that he has given us a different religion? . . .
>
> Brother! We do not wish to destroy your religion, or take it from you. We only want to enjoy our own.

2 THE BUNDLE OF TWIGS

My cause will not die, when I am dead.

Tecumseh (Shawnee)

As the white settlers pushed north and west in the mid-eighteenth century, they threatened the homelands of the Algonquian peoples, such as the Delaware, the Kickapoo, and the Potawatomi. This encroachment was fiercely resisted by Algonquian leaders, most effectively by Pontiac of the Ottawa Nation.

Pontiac was a war chief of such stature that the campaign he waged against the settlers in 1763–66 became known as "Pontiac's War." His forces killed more than two thousand settlers illegally squatting on Indian land, and took nine British forts. In retaliation, the British adopted a policy of genocide. Sir Jeffrey Amherst, the commander of the British forces, vowed "to punish the delinquents with entire destruction." On his orders, the Delawares besieging Fort Pitt (at Pittsburgh, Pennsylvania) were invited inside for talks and presented with gifts of blankets infected with the smallpox virus.

Using the word "inoculate" in the sense of "infect," Amherst had written to Colonel Henry Bouquet, "You will do well to inoculate the Indians by means of blankets, as well as to try every other method that can serve to extirpate this execrable race." Neither Amherst nor Bouquet had any qualms about unleashing biological terror on the Native Americans, whom they regarded as "vermin." They were sorry only that it was not practical to hunt them down with dogs.

Smallpox epidemics raged among the Ohio nations

David Octavius Hill and Robert Adamson
Kahkewaquonaby
1845

This is the first photograph ever taken of a Native American. Kahkewaquonaby (1802-56) was a Mississauga Ojibwe from Canada. He converted to Methodist Christianity and became a missionary, better known under the name the Rev. Peter Jones. He wrote a History of the Ojebway Indians, *and after his death the Wesleyan Missionary Committee published his* Life and Journals.

allied to Pontiac—the Delaware, the Mingo, the Shawnee, and Pontiac's own people, the Ottawa—and effectively crushed their resistance. An Ottawa historian, Andrew Blackbird, recorded the orally transmitted folk memory of this terrible time in a book published in 1887.

> The Ottawas were greatly reduced in numbers on account of the smallpox. . . . This smallpox was sold to them shut up in a tin box, with the strict injunction not to open their box on their way homeward, but only when they should reach their country; and that this box contained something that would do them great good, and their people! . . . Accordingly, after they reached home they opened the box: but behold there was another tin box inside, smaller . . . and when they opened the last one they found nothing but mouldy particles in this last little box! . . . But alas, alas! pretty soon burst out a terrible sickness among them.

That a genuine historic tragedy should be interpreted in the terms of a myth or folktale is not surprising. Religious beliefs are central to the history of Native American resistance to white rule. While to the British Pontiac's War was a military campaign, to the Native Americans it was essentially a spiritual one. It was the visions and prophecies of the Delaware holy man Neolin that united the Seneca, Ottawa, Delaware, Ojibwe, and others in armed resistance to the British, under Pontiac's military leadership.

In 1762 Neolin had made a spirit journey to the land of the Master of Life, the god who is in charge of all souls, both human and animal. There he was asked, "The land on which you are, I have made for you, not for others: why do you suffer the whites to dwell upon your lands?" Because the Indians were becoming corrupted by the white man's ways and the white man's weapons, the Master of Life had withdrawn the game animals into the depths of the forest. This theme of the Master of Life withholding and releasing game was deeply ingrained in Native American religion.

The way in which Neolin's vision united tribes behind Pontiac was to be repeated on a grander scale in the early years of the nineteenth century, when an even broader coalition grew around the Shawnee war leader Tecumseh and his brother Tenskwatawa, often known simply as "the Prophet." Although it is Tecumseh (sometimes spelled Tecumthe) who has gained lasting fame as one of the greatest of all Native Americans, he first came to the white man's attention simply as "the brother of the Prophet."

Tenskwatawa worried the whites, for he, like Neolin, had been vouchsafed a great vision by the Master of Life. The Prophet was a traditional healer or medicine man, but not a highly respected figure among the Shawnee; he had a reputation as an idler and a drunkard. His great vision changed all that, and soon Indians were flocking to hear his message.

In a trance, the Prophet's spirit had traveled the path of the dead until he reached a crossroads. To the right lay the path to heaven; to the left, the path to a house named Eternity, where the souls of the sinful were suffering such torments that the Prophet could hear them "roaring like the falls of a river."

In this fearful vision, elements of the Christian heaven and hell are combined with the traditional Algonquian and Iroquoian belief in a Good Spirit and an Evil Spirit (imagined by both the Shawnee and the Delaware as a gigantic water serpent).

After receiving his vision, the Prophet was a transformed man. He abandoned his old name Lalawéthika, the Rattle, and became Tenskwatawa, the Open Door. The Prophet saw himself literally as a door through which the Indians could pass into a better world. Many of his followers regarded him as a reincarnation of the great mythical teacher of mankind Winabojo (sometimes spelled Manobozho).

after Charles Bird King
Tenskwatawa
1835–36

An old accident left Tenskwatawa blind in the right eye; this closed eye accentuated the naturally mournful cast of his features. His guardian spirits called him to be a healer at a young age, but until his great vision he lived a dissolute life. Governor William Henry Harrison played on this knowledge to undermine Tenskwatawa's influence, asking the Delawares, "Who is this pretended prophet who dares to speak in the name of the Great Creator?"

21

Tenskwatawa told all who would listen of the great revelation he had been granted by the Master of Life.
Essentially, his message was the same as the one Neolin
had preached to an earlier generation: The Indians must
renounce the white man's ways—his whiskey, his guns, his
foodstuffs, and his clothes—and return to their own traditions. But there were also changes to those traditions. In
particular, Tenskwatawa required his followers to throw
away their sacred medicine bags (and with them the protection of their guardian spirits) and rely only on him as
their guide and protector. This, he said, was to prevent
sorcery and witchcraft, which the Indians regarded as the
primary source of the epidemics that were still devastating
their communities.

Tenskwatawa sent emissaries bearing his message to all
the tribes of the Great Lakes, and later even as far as Plains
nations such as the Blackfoot. These disciples, speaking on
the Prophet's behalf, carried with them a life-size effigy of
the Prophet himself, with his sacred fire in his right hand
and four mystic strings of beans in the left, to which converts could make their vows. Drawing the strings of beans
through your hands was called "shaking hands with the
Prophet." According to the Ojibwe historian William
Warren, such was the excitement at the Prophet's message
of hope that the shores of Lake Superior were strewn with
discarded medicine bags.

Converts were told to light a fire with two dry sticks and
make sure it never went out. In four years, they were told,
the Great Spirit would cover the land in darkness, sweep
away the white men, release the game, and restore the
dead to life.

The message was resolutely antiwhite. The Great
Spirit—speaking through Tenskwatawa, who was the "first
man" (that is, Winabojo, or, in Shawnee terms, Cloudy Boy)
brought back to life—declared:

> The Americans I did not make. They are not my children, but the children of the Evil Spirit. They grew from the scum of the great water, when it was troubled by the Evil Spirit, and the froth was driven into the woods by a strong east wind. They are numerous, but I hate them. They are unjust. They have taken your lands, which were not made for them.

Yet the Prophet's message was one of peace rather than war. He told his listeners they need not worry about the Americans. If he so wished, he boasted, he could ask the great turtle that the Shawnee believe supports the land to flip over and spill the whites like water from a basin.

While Tenskwatawa was preaching peace, his brother Tecumseh was preparing for war. The believers from many tribes who flocked to hear the words of the Prophet absorbed not just the idea of a coming apocalypse, from which the Indians would emerge triumphant, but also a new sense of pan-Indian unity. Summoned to account for himself to the governor of the Indiana Territory, William Henry Harrison, in 1808, Tenskwatawa told him:

> The religion which I have established for the last three years has been attended to by the different tribes of Indians. Those Indians were once different people. They are now but one. They are all determined to practice what I have communicated to them that has come immediately from the Great Spirit through me.

The quest for pan-Indian unity was not new. Through the second half of the eighteenth century there had been a "Nativist" movement with precisely that aim, and in this movement the Shawnee had always been prominent. They had even established a kind of semipermanent "embassy" system among other Indian nations.

Why the Shawnee, who had already lost most of their tribal lands and were scattered and demoralized, should have taken the lead is directly related to their religious beliefs.

after Charles Bird King
Quatawapea 1835–36

Also known as Lewis, Quatawapea was the head of a band of Ohio Shawnees and Mingoes. He is shown wearing a medal he received from President Jefferson in 1802; these "Peace medals" were highly prized by Indian chiefs, and played a part in preventing hostilities. Nevertheless, Quatawapea was an early convert to Tecumseh's cause; perhaps he belonged to the turtle clan, the clan of Tecumseh's mother.

The Shawnee believed that this world was created by an old woman named Kokumthena, Our Grandmother, also known as Snaggle Tooth Woman or Cloud, who had descended from the sky world. After her wicked grandson, the water serpent that embodies the Evil Spirit, destroyed the world with a flood, she remade it. Our Grandmother and her good grandson, Cloudy Boy, created the Shawnee and taught them how to live. Then she went to live in the moon, where she can still be seen bending over her cooking pot during a full moon.

Tenskwatawa seems to have tried to obscure the fact that the Shawnee Creator was female. In the version of Shawnee mythology recorded by C. C. Trowbridge, for which Tenskwatawa was the main informant, Our Grandmother is reduced to a supporting role, and it is stressed that no being except the Great Spirit was to be credited with the Creation. This brought Shawnee belief more closely into line with that of the other nations, a necessary step toward a successful intertribal religion. In many accounts the role of Our Grandmother is attributed to a masculine Great Spirit.

The Shawnee were the first humans on the new earth, and the Creator even gave them a portion of his—or her—own heart in the sacred medicine bundle of the tribe. This medicine bundle, said to contain an everlasting fire, was kept in its own lodge, in the safekeeping of the holy men of the Mekoches, the first of the five divisions of the Shawnee made by the Creator, and therefore the most senior. No doubt Tenskwatawa would have dearly loved to have access to this medicine bundle, but he and Tecumseh were members, through their father, of the junior Kispoko division. The image of himself that Tenskwatawa sent out with his disciples was, in a way, a new version of the sacred medicine bundle that gave the Shawnee their claim to pre-eminence among the Indian nations. As one Shawnee put

Fleury Generelly
Shawnee camp on the Mississippi River
1820

The numbers on this sketch of a temporary Shawnee encampment indicate: 1, a pole shelter with a bark roof and leaf or brush floor; 2, a cradle; 3, a log pestle and mortar for grinding corn; 4, a deerskin stretched for drying.

it, "The Great Spirit . . . ordered that everything upon the earth should obey us. . . . He put his heart right into our tribe and made it the chief of all tribes. . . . We think we have a right to look upon ourselves as the head tribe of all nations."

Tecumseh's name is hard to translate, but it means something like "spirit panther leaping like a shooting star across the skies." Everyone who met him agreed he was a dazzling figure. Governor William Henry Harrison compared him to Moses; the British commander in Upper Canada, Major General Isaac Brock, compared him to the greatest British soldier of the time, describing him as "the Wellington of the Indians." The Shawnee themselves remembered him simply as "the bravest man that ever was."

One of Isaac Brock's aides, Captain John B. Glegg, set down a vivid description of Tecumseh in his prime.

> Tecumseh's appearance was very prepossessing; his figure light and finely proportioned; his age I imagined to be about five and thirty; in height, five feet nine or ten inches; his complexion, light copper; countenance, oval, with bright hazel eyes beaming cheerfulness, energy and decision. Three small silver crowns, or coronets, were suspended from the lower cartilage of his aquiline nose; and a large silver medallion of George the Third . . . was attached to a mixed colored wampum string, and hung round his neck. His dress consisted of a plain, neat uniform, tanned deerskin jacket, with long trousers of the same material, the seams of both being covered with neatly cut fringe; and he had on his feet leather moccasins, much ornamented with work made from the dyed quills of the porcupine.

Tecumseh is thought to have been born in 1768, so he was probably forty-four when he first met Brock and Glegg in 1812. His childhood had been marked by conflict and tragedy, and he was raised to be a warrior. His father was slain in a battle with British troops in 1774, and Tecumseh was brought up by his sister Tecumapease, under the guidance of his older brother, Chiksika.

Chiksika's temperament is well demonstrated by a speech he made at a war council called by the Cherokee in 1792. A chief named Bloody Fellow argued eloquently for peace with the Americans. Then Chiksika rose to his feet and, stretching out his hands toward Bloody Fellow, said, "With these hands, I have taken the lives of three hundred men, and now the time is come when they shall take the lives of three hundred more. Then I will be satisfied, and sit down in peace. I will now drink my fill of blood." Within a month Chiksika himself was dead. His loss was devastating to Tecumseh, who had looked up to his brother and fought alongside him.

Tecumseh became both the war chief and peace chief of

his people. The two roles were usually kept separate but could be combined in the hands of an exceptional man, which Tecumseh had proved himself to be. And it was from this position, as chief of a junior division of the Shawnee, that Tecumseh set himself, with relentless drive and determination, to unite the Native American nations, from Mexico to the Great Lakes. By 1810 he could boast with some truth, "I am alone the acknowledged head of all the Indians."

If one event shaped Tecumseh's political vision, it was the Treaty of Greenville, signed in 1795, in which the Shawnee and others ceded to the United States two-thirds of the state of Ohio for a pittance. This was the end result of the long struggle in which both Tecumseh's father and his beloved brother had lost their lives.

Tecumseh's reaction was both bitter and forceful.

> My heart is a stone: heavy with sadness for my people; cold with the knowledge that no treaty will keep the whites out of our lands; hard with the determination to resist as long as I live and breathe. Now we are weak and many of our people are afraid. But hear me: a single twig breaks, but the bundle of twigs is strong. Someday I will embrace our brother tribes and draw them into a bundle and together we will win our country back from the whites.

The bundle of twigs was more than a metaphor for Tecumseh: It was to become an essential part of his military strategy. Bundles of sticks, painted red for war, were left with the various tribes. Each day one stick was to be removed. When the last stick was reached, it was time to act. In this way Tecumseh tried to ensure that unity of purpose was translated into unity of action. But again and again his plans were disrupted by hotheads who could not wait until the agreed time before launching an attack.

As early as 1772, Shawnee leaders had urged other tribes

to the north, west, and south of their territories to unite with them. The Indians, they argued, should "be all of one mind and of one color." Men such as the Shawnee war chiefs Cornstalk and Blue Jacket offered the young Tecumseh models of determination and diplomacy. But it was the Mohawk leader Joseph Brant who first articulated in 1783 what was to become Tecumseh's central philosophy—that all the land belonged to the Indian nations in common and could not be sold off piecemeal by particular tribes or individuals. Tecumseh was to make this point forcefully to Governor Harrison. The only way to stop the continual encroachment of the whites on Indian territory, he said, "is for all the red men to unite in claiming a common and equal right in the land. . . . Any sale not made by all is not valid."

What made Tecumseh's unifying vision so vital was the spiritual underpinning provided by the teachings of his brother Tenskwatawa. While the head chief of the Shawnee, Black Hoof, accepted government aid to "civilize" the tribe and turn its menfolk into farmers rather than warriors and hunters, Tecumseh and Tenskwatawa offered a radical alternative: a complete return to the old ways.

On the upper Wabash, a few miles below the mouth of the Tippecanoe River in northwestern Indiana, the brothers established a new political and spiritual capital for the Shawnee, known to the whites as Prophetstown (near present-day Lafayette). From here their message of renewal through unity traveled far and wide.

With war looming between the British in Canada and the United States, both sides attempted to woo Tecumseh to their cause, and he in turn tried to keep in with both sides without committing himself. In the summer of 1809, things came to a crisis. Governor Harrison was determined to go ahead with yet another land treaty; Tecumseh angrily thrust the governor's letter into the fire.

Anon.
Tecumseh
19th century

No completely authentic portrait of Tecumseh exists. A painting once thought to be of Tecumseh is now generally believed to be of his son, Paukeesaa, while this engraving mistakenly shows Tecumseh in a British uniform.

In the treaty of Fort Wayne, Indiana, some three million acres of Indian territory were ceded to Governor Harrison for less than two cents an acre by representatives of the Potawatomi, Wea, Miami, and others. It was not until August 14, 1810, two weeks after the treaty was concluded, that Harrison himself first met Tecumseh. Harrison, who was seated on a raised dais, offered Tecumseh a seat beside him. In a move that stunned those present into silence, Tecumseh instead sat down on the grass, telling the governor that "the earth was the most proper place for the Indians, as they liked to repose upon the bosom of their mother."

Tecumseh used all his famous eloquence on the governor, and openly warned him that if Indian land rights were not respected, "I do not see how we can remain at peace with you." Harrison stood his ground. He defended the land treaties as both just and legal. The Indians were not one people, he said, nor did they hold the land in common. Tecumseh rose to his feet in a rage. Harrison, he said, was a liar. For a tense moment, violence was in the air.

By the next day Tecumseh had calmed down. Nevertheless, he warned Harrison that if he went ahead with the Fort Wayne Treaty, he must blame himself for the consequences. At a private meeting a few days later, Harrison promised to suspend the survey of the newly purchased land and present Tecumseh's case to President James Madison, the Great Chief, though he doubted it would achieve Tecumseh's purpose. Tecumseh replied:

> Well, as the Great Chief is to determine the matter, I hope the Great Spirit will put some sense into his head to induce him to direct you to give up this land. It is true, he is so far off. He will not be injured by the war. He may still sit in his town, and drink his wine, whilst you and I will have to fight it out.

Harrison and Tecumseh were fated to be enemies, yet each respected the other. Harrison wrote of Tecumseh that he was "one of those uncommon geniuses which spring up occasionally to produce revolutions and overturn the established order of things."

Through 1810 and 1811, Tecumseh busied himself melding the scattered nations into a united fighting force that would mass on the Wabash and forcibly defend the lands of the Fort Wayne Treaty. Alarmed by all this activity, Governor Harrison offered to send Tecumseh and the Prophet to Washington, with a guarantee of safe passage, to speak with the president himself. Tecumseh declined and calmly informed Harrison of the huge numbers of Indians from many different nations, especially Potawatomis, Kickapoos, Winnebagos, Wyandots, and Iroquois, who would soon be joining him on the Wabash. He did not complain, he said, about the various American states joining together in one confederacy, "nor should his white brothers complain of him for doing the same thing with regard to the Indian tribes."

Having united the northern tribes, Tecumseh left for the south, hoping to achieve the same among the Cherokee, Creek, and Choctaw. There he preached a message of coming cataclysm. Shortly after, the land was rocked by a series of devastating earthquakes, and soon it was being said not only that Tecumseh had predicted these, but even that he had caused them. The Creeks of Tukabahchee, Alabama, it was said, had doubted Tecumseh's message. He had told them that he was heading north, and that when he reached Detroit he would stamp his foot on the ground and shake down every house in Tukabahchee. When an earthquake destroyed their village, the Creeks were in no doubt that Tecumseh had arrived in Detroit.

Tecumseh certainly seized on the earthquakes as evidence of the Great Spirit's wish to rid the land of the whites. He told the fierce Osage:

> Brothers, the Great Spirit is angry with our enemies. He speaks in thunder, and the earth swallows up villages, and drinks up the Mississippi. The great waters will cover their lowlands. Their corn cannot grow, and the Great Spirit will sweep those who escape to the hills from the earth with his terrible breath.

While Tecumseh was making his grand tour of the south, and paving the way for the Red Stick War of 1813, Governor Harrison was taking steps to undo what Tecumseh had already achieved in the north. With a thousand troops, Harrison attacked Prophetstown. The ensuing battle of Tippecanoe was a fierce and bloody one in which the Indians, urged on by Tenskwatawa, inflicted serious damage on Harrison's force, killing sixty-eight of his men. But when it was over, Harrison burned Prophetstown to the ground. The granaries of corn intended to last Tecumseh's people through the winter were consumed by the flames.

Josiah Francis
Self-portrait
1816

Josiah Francis, or Medicine Maker, was part Creek. He became the Red Stick prophet, preaching a warlike version of Tenskwatawa's religion.

Tecumseh was furious that his brother had not managed to avoid violence. "Had I been at home and heard of the advance of the American troops towards our village," he said, "I should have gone to meet them, and shaking them by the hand, have asked them the reason of their appearance in such hostile guise." The battle of Tippecanoe itself he dismissed as "a struggle between little children who only scratch each other's faces."

By the spring of 1812, war seemed inevitable. And just as Tecumseh rallied his troops to fight the Americans, so too war loomed between the United States and the British in Canada. On June 18, war was declared, and Tecumseh allied himself with the British, under the command of Major General Isaac Brock. The situation looked very bad for the British, outnumbered and ill supplied. Brock's solution was similar to Tecumseh's: He resolved to "speak loud and look big."

The two leaders were well suited to work together, especially since they were pitted against an American commander, Brigadier General William Hull, whose nickname among his own troops was "the Old Lady." In contrast, when Tecumseh met Brock, he is said to have turned to his people and exclaimed, "Ho-yo-o-e! This is a man!"

Tecumseh's constant guerrilla raids got Hull jumpy and nervous; Tecumseh's Indians seemed to be everywhere. By the time Brock and Tecumseh together besieged Detroit, Hull was ready to believe anything. In a simple ruse, Tecumseh marched his men in circles, passing through an opening in the woods visible from the fort, to convince Hull that he was surrounded by a vast force of savage Indians. Hull meekly surrendered the fort and the town, together with the whole of Michigan Territory, a quantity of guns and ammunition, a brand-new warship, and his entire force of 2,188 men.

It was an unqualified victory, in which Tecumseh and his

force of about 530 men had played a bold part. By supporting Brock's forces, Tecumseh had helped save Canada, and for this he is regarded in Canada as a national hero. But Tecumseh's alliance with the British was a matter of convenience rather than conviction. He was fighting against the Americans, not for Canada.

Isaac Brock both valued and admired Tecumseh, and he did what he could to support the Shawnee's wider aims. He argued both to the British prime minister, Robert Jenkinson (Lord Liverpool), and the governor-general of Canada, Sir George Prevost, that the peace negotiations with the United States should support the Indians' claim "to an extensive tract of country, fraudulently usurped from them." Prevost agreed. For a time, Tecumseh's dream seemed within his grasp.

But then it began to slip away. The Americans, sheltered in their military forts and fortified blockhouses, were able to resist the attacks of hostile Indians. The British, brimful of confidence from their recent successes, started to make mistakes. And in October 1812 Tecumseh's staunchest ally, Isaac Brock, was killed at the Battle of Queenston Heights.

The man who stepped into Brock's shoes, Colonel Henry Procter, was both less flexible and less resolute than his predecessor. Nevertheless, on the banks of the Raisin River in Michigan, he inflicted a crushing defeat on the American forces commanded by James Winchester. This was one of three armies under the overall command of William Henry Harrison, whose chief aim was to recapture Detroit. Procter retreated victorious, with 592 American prisoners. He left 80 American wounded behind, promising to send transport to collect them. Instead, these vulnerable men, who should have been under Procter's protection, were massacred by Native Americans celebrating the victory and claiming revenge for their own lost warriors. The slaughter of the prisoners, added to the shame

Anon.
Battle of the Thames—death of Tecumseh
19th century

Tecumseh was described by an eyewitness, John Richardson, moving along the British line to hearten the troops: "He was dressed in his usual deer skin dress, which admirably displayed his light yet sinewy figure, and in his handkerchief, rolled as a turban over his brow, was placed a handsome white ostrich feather." This engraving portrays the most popular version of Tecumseh's death, in which he is shot by the commander of the Kentucky mounted volunteers, Richard Mentor Johnson. Johnson used his claim to have killed Tecumseh to further his political career, and it helped him to the vice presidency in 1837.

of the earlier surrender of Detroit, stiffened American resolve. "Remember the Raisin!" became a rallying cry.

Tecumseh was not present at the Raisin. If he had been, the needless massacre of American wounded would probably have been avoided. Tecumseh, though an implacable adversary in war, was noted for his courteous treatment of captives. He argued strongly against traditional practices such as the burning of prisoners and, where he was able to do so, actively prevented them.

When Tecumseh rejoined Procter in April 1813, they launched an attack on Harrison in Fort Meigs, Ohio. The Americans dug in and could not be overwhelmed. However, Tecumseh played a major part in forcing the surrender of eight hundred reinforcements under Colonel William Dudley. Then once again it seemed as if triumph was to be stained by slaughter. Word reached Tecumseh that the American prisoners, held in the ruins of Fort Miami, Ohio, were being massacred.

Tecumseh arrived at the scene, visibly angry and distressed, and quelled the violence by the force of his personality alone. The Canadian novelist John Richardson, who was a fifteen-year-old volunteer with the 41st Regiment of Foot, recalled the scene in his memoirs, and wrote, "Never did Tecumseh shine more truly than on this occasion." One account by a British officer has Tecumseh rebuking Procter for failing to halt the killing, and dismissing him disdainfully with the words, "Begone! You are unfit to command. Go and put on petticoats!"

This incident set the seal on Tecumseh's legend. That he was noble, generous, and brave is undisputed. It was Procter's misfortune that, to emphasize Tecumseh's greatness, the ineffectual British commander was depicted as an untrustworthy coward. As the tide of war turned, the British under Procter suffered a series of setbacks. The last of these, the defeat of the British fleet on Lake Erie on

September 10, 1813, caused Procter to prepare his retreat.

A week later Tecumseh, sensing that Procter was about to abandon him and unaware of the scale of the defeat, compared Procter to "a fat animal that carries its tail upon its back, but when affrighted, it drops it between its legs and runs off." Tecumseh used all his rhetorical skill to plead with Procter not to give up.

> Listen, Father! The Americans have not yet defeated us by land; neither are we sure they have done so by water. We, therefore, wish to remain here, and fight our enemy should they make their appearance. . . . Our lives are in the hands of the Great Spirit. We are determined to defend our lands, and if it is his will, we wish to leave our bones upon them.

Despite Tecumseh's eloquence, Procter would not make a stand. Instead, he persuaded Tecumseh to abandon Fort Malden, at the head of Lake Erie, and retreat with him to the forks of the Thames. Procter went ahead, supposedly to prepare a defensive position, but when Tecumseh

James Westhall Ford
The Winnebago prophet, Black Hawk, and Whirling Thunder 1833

The career of the Sac warrior Black Hawk (Makataimeshekiakiak, 1767–1838) illustrates the internal rivalries that prevented many Indian nations from effective opposition to the United States. An astute military strategist, Black Hawk distinguished himself fighting alongside the British in the War of 1812, but was overlooked as the Sac war leader in favor of the more eloquent and statesmanlike Keokuk. He became the spokesman for a band of Sacs, Mesquakies, Winnebagos, and Foxes who refused to be removed to the west; when he led this so-called British Band east into Illinois, he sparked the Black Hawk War of 1832. His warriors were slaughtered, and Black Hawk himself was taken prisoner and disgraced. He is pictured here with his son Whirling Thunder and his spiritual adviser White Cloud, "the Winnebago prophet," who was actually of mixed Winnebago and Sac descent. Influenced by White Cloud, Black Hawk pronounced, "My reason teaches me that land cannot be sold."

arrived, nothing had been done. Dithering and disheartened, Procter had changed his mind and retreated several miles farther up the Thames, to Moraviantown.

There, on October 5, 1813, Procter had to stand and fight. He had about 450 tired and dispirited soldiers under his command; Tecumseh, a similar number of hardened warriors. Their joint forces were outnumbered by three to one. Almost immediately, the Americans smashed through the British lines, and Procter himself fled on horseback.

Tecumseh held firm and engaged the enemy. He rallied his troops and encouraged them by thrusting himself into the thick of the action. As he sprang forward, one of the Americans shot him in the chest. While the news spread that Tecumseh was dead, the Indians melted from the battlefield. Tecumseh's war was over.

The realities of a military campaign had already overshadowed the visionary fervor of Tecumseh's brother Tenskwatawa. Now the Prophet's influence dwindled away. The Shawnee, it is true, elected him their new war chief, but the war had effectively ended. And with the peace came the knowledge that despite all the efforts of Tecumseh's confederacy, the northeastern nations had not retrieved a single acre of the land they had lost, while the southeastern nations, compromised by their support of Tecumseh, were on the brink of losing everything they held dear.

Over the coming years, several charismatic individuals inherited some of Tecumseh's mantle, but none of them had quite the balance of passion and vision to unite the Indian nations that Tecumseh had. One by one they foundered in wars they could not win: Black Hawk, the Sac leader in the Black Hawk War of 1832; Osceola, the Seminole leader in the Second Seminole War of 1835; Kamiakin, the Yakama leader in the Yakima War of 1855–58; Sitting Bull, the Lakota holy man and war chief in the Great Sioux War of 1876.

Yet through all the defeats that were to come, something of Tecumseh's spirit survived. The Ghost Dance movement of the late 1880s was one of many movements of spiritual renewal and Native American unity to draw inspiration from the same well as Tecumseh and Tenskwatawa. Subsequently, the struggles for cultural equality, social justice, and religious freedom have continued right to the present day, with organizations such as the Native American Church, the National Congress of American Indians, and the American Indian Movement (AIM) continuing to fight for the same principles for which Tecumseh died.

3 THE TRAIL OF TEARS

I saw a trail to the big river
and then I cried.

Choctaw song
translated by Muriel Hazel Wright

The crushing of Tecumseh's pan-Indian movement marks the last point at which the Native Americans could conceivably have united in real strength to oppose white settlement. In the bitter aftermath, the southeastern nations Tecumseh had tried to rally to his cause were dispossessed of their lands and their independence.

The southeast was one of the most fertile and hospitable regions of North America, home to some of the most settled and prosperous peoples. They lived by hunting and fishing, gathering wild plants, and cultivating crops such as corn, beans, and squash.

The first major contact between these peoples and the whites was the disastrous expedition of the ruthless Spaniard Hernando de Soto in 1539–43. This was also their first contact with a range of European diseases. The ensuing epidemics came in waves that decimated nation after nation. In 1738–39 a smallpox outbreak in the Cherokee Nation, the largest in the southeast, killed nearly half the population.

The smaller nations dwindled and disappeared, or merged with their neighbors, until by the nineteenth century there were only five major groupings in the region, often patronizingly referred to by whites as the "Five Civilized Tribes." These were the Cherokee, Choctaw, Chickasaw, Seminole, and Creek nations.

Anon.
Seminole man
19th century

The Seminole, a Muskogean people partly descended from the original Florida tribes destroyed by first contact with the whites, were considered one of the "Five Civilized Tribes." However, the word Seminole, *derived from the Spanish* cimarrón, *means "wild." This man wears elaborate traditional dress very much like that sported by Osceola, the Seminole war leader in the Second Seminole War, which started in 1835. Osceola was fiercely opposed to land sales to the whites, though he himself was the son of a white trader, William Powell. His last wish before he died in 1838 was to be dressed in his finest clothes.*

As white settlers moved into the traditional territories of these peoples, they found it necessary time and time again to reach an accommodation with the original inhabitants. The first treaty between the English colonists in South Carolina and the Cherokee was signed in 1648. In this treaty, as in every subsequent one, the Cherokee gave the whites land and the whites gave the Cherokee empty promises.

Some whites did live on genuinely friendly terms with the Indians. Traders, in particular, often took Indian wives and were accepted into the tribe. Cornelius Dougherty, an Irishman from Virginia, was the first trader to establish himself among the Cherokee, in 1690, and his descendants can still be traced in the Cherokee Nation today.

In many cases, however, the settlers were driven more by greed than by friendship. In 1705 the Cherokee complained to Governor James Moore of South Carolina about the whites who were conspiring "to set upon, assault, kill, destroy, and take captive as many Indians as they possibly could." But since these white men had received commissions from the governor himself to act in this way, and the captured Indians were sold into slavery for his and their private profit, complaint was useless.

The great forward thrust of "civilization" was unstoppable. Therefore, the whites argued, the only future for the Native Americans was to become "civilized." After a number of futile wars followed by forced and unsatisfactory treaties in which they ceded more and more of their land to the whites, even the Indians themselves began to accept this argument. After the first Treaty of Tellico, North Carolina, in 1798—in which thirty-nine Cherokee chiefs surrendered yet more land to the United States in return for five thousand dollars in goods, one thousand dollars a year, and the usual promise to "continue the guarantee of the remainder of their country forever"—the unequal armed struggle to preserve Cherokee territory was over. From then on, the Cherokee would rely on argument and diplomacy rather than the tomahawk in their fight for survival.

By a treaty of 1791 the government had agreed to furnish the Cherokee with farming tools, spinning wheels, looms, and so on, in pursuit of this "civilizing" policy. The policy was enthusiastically embraced by many Cherokees, particularly those in the lowlands, where many of the most prominent families—for instance, the Doughertys, the Rosses, and the Waffords—were of mixed blood. The full-blooded mountain Cherokees were more conservative.

In 1801 the first mission to the Cherokee was opened by two Moravian ministers, followed by a school. By 1812 the Cherokee were well on their way to "civilization." It was in that year that Tecumseh's message of Indian renewal reached them, via the Creeks, who had embraced it enthusiastically. A prophet named Tsali preached Tenskwatawa's new religion to the Cherokee at a great medicine dance held at Ustanali, Georgia, the national capital. His words are summarized by the ethnologist James Mooney:

> The Cherokees had broken the road which had been given to their fathers at the beginning of the world. They had taken the white man's clothes and trinkets, they had beds and tables and mills; some even had books and cats. All this was bad, and because of it their gods were angry and the game was leaving their country. If they would live and be happy as before, they must put off the white man's dress, throw away his mills and looms, kill their cats, put on paint and buckskin, and be Indians again; otherwise swift destruction would come upon them.

The listeners were highly excited by this news. A prominent chief, Major Ridge, warned them that such a course would lead to war, but "the maddened followers of the prophet sprang upon Ridge and would have killed him but for the interposition of friends."

after Charles Bird King
Major Ridge 1835–36

Major Ridge (c.1771–1839), the head of the Treaty faction, was one of the most eloquent of the Cherokee leaders. In a speech given during treaty negotiations at New Echota in 1835 he said:"We can never forget these homes, I know, but an unbending, iron necessity tells us we must leave them. I would willingly die to preserve them, but any forcible effort to keep them will cost us our lands, our lives and the lives of our children. There is but one path to safety, one road to future existence as a Nation. That path is open before you. Make a treaty of cession. Give up these lands and go over beyond the great Father of Waters."

Believing that a terrible storm was coming that would destroy all but the true believers, many Cherokees abandoned all the trappings of civilization—"their bees, their orchards, their slaves, and everything that had come to them from the white man"—and took refuge on the high summits of the Great Smoky Mountains. James Wafford, a Cherokee who was then about ten years old, remembered the pilgrims, with packs on their backs, trudging up to await the day of doom. When it did not arrive, they made the sad journey down from the North Carolina mountaintops to their homes in Alabama and Georgia.

The disappointed hopes of these humiliated believers, together with the influence of Major Ridge and other chiefs, probably saved the Cherokee from joining with the Creek in the Red Stick War, which began with the massacre of 107 soldiers, 160 civilians, and 100 slaves at Fort Mims, Alabama, on August 30, 1813.

Instead of aiding the Creek "Red Sticks" (as those allied with Tecumseh were called), the Cherokees under Ridge declared war upon them. Together with some friendly Creeks, Choctaws, and Chickasaws, the Cherokees served alongside the American armies under Generals White and Jackson.

General Andrew Jackson was to play a crucial role in Cherokee history. At this point, he was their ally and trusted friend. At the decisive battle of Horseshoe Bend, Alabama, the war skills of five hundred Cherokees among Jackson's command were crucial in turning a battle into a rout, in which almost the entire force of the Creek was destroyed. Of an estimated one thousand Creek warriors, Jackson reported that not more than twenty escaped alive; only three were taken prisoner. Major Ridge, whose counsel was among the factors that prevented the Cherokee from joining with the Creeks, earned the rank of major in this campaign.

The story of this chief's name is a study in miniature of the "civilizing" of the Cherokee. He was called Kahnungdatlageh, which means "Man Who Walks on the Mountain Top" in Cherokee. For simplicity, he himself shortened this to The Ridge. After the Creek War he added the title of major as a first name and became Major Ridge. His son, also prominent in the history of the Cherokees at this crucial time, was known simply as John Ridge, with his father's surname and a white man's forename. From the "savage" Kahnungdatlageh to the "civilized" John Ridge took only a generation.

John Ridge was born in 1803 and educated first at the Moravian mission school, then by private tutor, and lastly at the American Board's Foreign Mission School in Cornwall, Connecticut. "Civilization" seemed well within his grasp; he even fell in love with and married Sarah Northrup, the daughter of the Foreign Mission School's white steward.

But all was not plain sailing for this romance. The editor of the local newspaper, the Litchfield *American Eagle,* scandalized that Sarah had "made herself a *squaw,*" proclaimed that "the girl ought to be publicly whipped, the Indian hung, and the mother drowned." When, shortly afterward, John's cousin Elias Boudinot married another white girl from the town, Harriet Gold, feelings ran so high that Harriet's own brother set fire to her effigy on a funeral pyre while the church bells tolled mournfully across the green.

As a result of the furor, the Foreign Mission School had to close, but both marriages went ahead. John Ridge wrote a long letter on February 27, 1826, to the statesman Albert Gallatin, who had served in Thomas Jefferson's cabinet, outlining the current state of the Cherokee. He noted that intermarriage with the whites "has been increasing in proportion to the march of civilization."

after Charles Bird King
John Ridge 1835-36

John Ridge was to be murdered along with his father, Major Ridge, and Elias Boudinot on June 22, 1839, an act of revenge by elements of the Ross faction for their part in negotiating the 1835 Treaty of New Echota. A party of twenty-five men was sent to his house to murder him at dawn.
See pp. 51-54.

An official census of 1835 lists 12,776 Cherokees—just over three-quarters of the nation—as "full bloods." These included many of the mountain Cherokees. But among the lowland Cherokees an upper class of mixed-blood families was emerging. These people embraced white ideas of civilization and imitated the gracious lifestyle of their white neighbors on southern plantations. This included such niceties as eating regular meals at a well-laid table, as well as the ownership of black slaves. In John Ridge's words:

> The African slaves are generally mostly held by Half breeds and full Indians of distinguished talents. In this class the principal value of property is retained and their farms are conducted in the same style with the southern white farmers of equal ability in point of property. Their houses are usually of hewed logs, with brick chimneys & shingled roofs, there are also a few excellent Brick houses & frames. Their furniture is better than the exterior appearance of their houses would incline a stranger to suppose. They have their regular meals as the whites, Servants to attend them in their repasts, and the tables are usually covered with a clean cloth & furnished with the usual plates, knives & forks &c.

Ridge reckoned that in 1826 the Cherokee Nation comprised 15,480 souls, including 1,277 African American slaves. The Cherokee, like other tribes, had treated captives from war raids as slaves of a sort, but slaveholding on this scale was a direct imitation of the white society of the day. Many traditional Cherokees disapproved of it, and this division between those who owned slaves and those who did not was to widen into a fearful rift in the dark days of the Civil War.

Slavery and table manners were not the only markers of civilization. The Cherokee had established their own government—in two houses in imitation of the U.S. system—with its own constitution. They published and enforced their own laws. They encouraged education and, with it, conversion to Christianity. They had largely abandoned their traditional hunting lifestyle and become farmers.

Most remarkable of all, the Cherokee had achieved almost universal literacy—at a time when many of their white neighbors could barely read or write. They had done this completely on their own, in one of the most astounding social transformations in human history. A completely oral culture became literate almost overnight.

The source of this remarkable change was the ingenuity of one man, Sequoyah, who was also known as George Gist (sometimes spelled Guest or Guess). Sequoyah knew no English but was intrigued by the idea that the whites could record speech on paper and interpret it whenever they wished, whereas Cherokee, like other Indian languages, had no written form. He devoted years to inventing a similar system for Cherokee. As he put it, in a typically Cherokee simile, "I thought that would be like catching a wild animal and taming it."

At first, Sequoyah devised a different symbol for each word, but he soon realized that this would not work. So he broke spoken Cherokee down into eighty-six syllables and assigned a symbol to each. Anyone who could speak Cherokee simply had to memorize these symbols and then could write it too.

Sequoyah finally completed his work in 1821. As James Mooney puts it, "Within a few months thousands of hitherto illiterate Cherokee were able to read and write their own language, teaching each other in the cabins and along the roadside." The new invention enabled the eastern Cherokees to communicate with those who had already emigrated west to Arkansas, where Sequoyah himself went to live in 1823.

Sequoyah's system for writing Cherokee had many profound effects on Cherokee civilization. On the one hand, it facilitated the spread of Christianity. A manuscript

after Charles Bird King
Sequoyah 1835–36

Sequoyah devoted twelve years of his life to the development of his unique method of writing Cherokee by reducing it to eighty-six, later eighty-five, characters, each representing a single syllable. The syllabary could be learned in a few weeks. In his later years, Sequoyah dreamed of inventing a universal Indian alphabet; he never learned to speak, read, or write the English language. He was born around 1770 and died in 1843.

ᏣᎳᎩ ᏧᎴᎯᏌᏅᎯ

CHEROKEE PHŒNIX,

VOL. I.   NEW ECHOTA, THURSDAY FEBRUARY 21, 1828.   **NO. 1.**

EDITED BY ELIAS BOUDINOTT.

PRINTED WEEKLY BY

ISAAC H. HARRIS,

FOR THE CHEROKEE NATION.

At $3 50 if paid in advance, $3 in six months, or $3 50 if paid at the end of the year.

To subscribers who can read only the Cherokee language the price will be $2,00 in advance, or $2,50 to be paid within the year.

Every subscription will be considered as continued unless subscribers give notice to the contrary before the commencement of a new year.

The Phoenix will be printed on a Super Royal sheet, with type entirely new procured for the purpose. Any person procuring six subscribers, and becoming responsible for the payment, shall receive a seventh gratis.

Advertisements will be inserted at seventy-five cents per square for the first insertion, and thirty-seven and a half cents for each continuance; longer ones in proportion.

☞ All letters addressed to the Editor, post paid, will receive due attention.

ᎧᏁᏌ ᎠᎦᏅᏬᎢ ᎠᏙ ᏂᏓᎦᎴᏅᏯ.

[Cherokee syllabary text]

A GOOD CONSCIENCE.

What is there, in all the pomp of the world, the enjoyments of luxury, or the gratification of passion, comparable to the tranquil delight of a good conscience? It is the feast of the mind. It is a sweet perfume, that diffuses its fragrance over every thing near it without exhausting its store. Compared with this, the gay pleasures of the world are like brilliants to a diamond eye, music to a deaf ear, wine in an ardent fever, or dainties in the languor of an ague. To lie down on the pillow, after a day spent in temperance in beneficence, and piety, how sweet is it! How different from the state of him, who reclines, at an unnatural hour, with his blood inflamed, his head throbbing with wine and gluttony, his heart aching with rancorous malice, his thoughts totally estranged from him who has protected him in the day, and will watch over him, ungrateful as he is, in the night season! A good conscience is, indeed, the peace of God. Passions lulled to sleep, clear thoughts, cheerful temper, a disposition to be pleased with every obvious and innocent object around; these are the effects of a good conscience; they are the things which constitute happiness; and these condensed to dwell with the poor man, in his humble cottage in the vale of obscurity. In the magnificent mansion of the proud and vain, glitter the exteriors of happiness, the gilding, the trapping, the pride and the pomp; but in the decent habitation of piety is oftener found the downy nest of heavenly peace; that solid good, of which the parade of the vain, the frivolous, and voluptuous, is but a shadowy semblance.

Christian Philosophy.

Flattery.—Few things are more universally condemned than flattery; yet there are few men, who are above its influence, and still fewer, who have courage sufficient to repel it with a faithful rebuke. The following anecdote is recommended, as affording a specimen of a good manner to flatterers. A certain clergyman in New England, eminent both for talents and humility, was one day accosted by a parishioner, who highly commended some of his performances, of which the clergyman himself had a very low opinion. After patiently hearing him a few moments, the clergyman replied; "My Friend, if I had not given me no better opinion of myself than I had before, but gives me much a worse opinion of you."

CONSTITUTION OF THE CHEROKEE NATION.

Formed by a Convention of Delegates from the several Districts, at New Echota, July 1827.

WE, THE REPRESENTATIVES of the people of the CHEROKEE NATION in Convention assembled, in order to establish justice, ensure tranquility, promote our common welfare, and secure to ourselves and our posterity the blessings of liberty; acknowledging with humility and gratitude the goodness of the sovereign Ruler of the Universe, in offering us an opportunity so favorable to the design, and imploring his aid and direction in its accomplishment, do ordain and establish this Constitution for the Government of the Cherokee Nation.

ARTICLE I.

SEC. 1. THE BOUNDARIES of this nation, embracing the lands solemnly guarantied and reserved forever to the Cherokee Nation by the Treaties concluded with the United States, are as follows; and shall forever hereafter remain unalterably the same—to wit—Beginning on the north Bank of Tennessee River at the upper part of the Chickasaw old fields; thence along the main channel of said river, including all the islands therein, to the mouth of the Hiwassee river, thence up the main channel of said river, including Islands, to the first hill which closes in on said river, about two miles above Hiwassee old Town; thence along the ridge which divides the waters of the Hiwassee and Little Tellico, to the Tennessee river at Tallassee; thence along the main channel, including Islands, to the junction of the Cowee and Nantayalee; thence along the ridge in the fork of said river, to the top of the blue ridge; thence along the blue ridge to the Unicoy Turnpike road; thence by a straight line to the main source of the Chestatee; thence along its main channel, including Islands, to the Chattahoochy; and thence down the same to the Creek boundary at Buzzard Roost; thence along the boundary line which separates this and the Creek Nation, to a point on the Coosa river opposite the mouth of Wills Creek; thence down along the South bank of the same to a point opposite to Fort Strother; thence up the river to the mouth of Wills Creek; thence up along the East bank of said creek, to the West branch thereof, and up the same to its source; and thence along the ridge which separates the Tombeebee and Tennessee waters, to a point on the top of said ridge; thence due North to Camp Coffee on Tennessee river, which is opposite the Chickasaw Island; and thence to the place of beginning.

SEC. 2. The Sovereignty and Jurisdiction of this Government shall extend over the Country within the boundaries above described, and the lands therein are, and shall remain, the common property of the Nation; but the improvements made thereon, and in the possession of the citizens of the Nation, are the exclusive and indefeasible property of the citizens respectively who made, or may rightfully be in possession of them; *Provided*, That the citizens of the Nation, possessing exclusive and indefeasible right to their respective improvements, as expressed in this article, shall possess no right nor power to dispose of their improvements in any manner whatever to the United States, individual States, nor to individual citizens thereof; and that, whenever any such citizen or citizens shall remove with their effects out of the limits of this Nation, and become citizens of any other Government, all their right and privileges as citizens of this Nation shall cease; *Provided nevertheless*, That the Legislature shall have power to re-admit by law to all the rights of citizenship, any such person or persons, who may at any time desire to return to the Nation on their memorializing the General Council for such

[Cherokee syllabary columns]

readmission. *Moreover*, the Legislature shall have power to adopt such laws and regulations, as its wisdom may deem expedient and proper, to prevent the citizens from monopolizing improvements with the view of speculation.

ARTICLE II.

SEC. 1. THE POWER of this Government shall be divided into three distinct departments;—the Legislative, the Executive, and the Judicial.

SEC. 2. No person or persons, belonging to one of these Departments, shall exercise any of the powers properly belonging to either of the others, except in the cases hereinafter expressly directed or permitted.

ARTICLE III.

SEC. 1. THE LEGISLATIVE POWER shall be vested in two distinct branches; a Committee, and a Council; each to have a negative on the other, and both to be styled, the General Council of the Cherokee Nation; and the style of their acts and laws shall be,

"Resolved by the Committee and Council in General Council convened."

SEC. 2. The Cherokee Nation, as laid off into eight Districts, shall so remain.

SEC. 3. The Committee shall consist of two members from each District, and the Council shall consist of three members from each District, to be chosen by the qualified electors of their respective Districts for two years; and the elections to be held in every District on the first Monday in August for the year 1828, and every succeeding two years thereafter; and the General Council shall be held once a year, to be convened on the second Monday of October in each year, at New Echota.

SEC. 4. No person shall be eligible to a seat in the General Council, but a free Cherokee Male citizen, who shall have attained to the age of twenty-five years. The descendants of Cherokee men by all free women, except the African race, whose parents may be or have been living together as man and wife, according to the customs and laws of this Nation, shall be entitled to all the rights and privileges of this Nation, as well as the posterity of Cherokee women by all free men. No person who is of negro or mulatto parentage, either by the father or mother side, shall be eligible to hold any office of profit, honor or trust, under this Government.

SEC. 5. The Electors, and members of the the General Council shall, in all cases except those of treason, felony, or breach of the peace, be privileged from arrest during their attendance at election, and at the General Council, and in going to, and returning from, the same.

SEC. 6. In all elections by the people, the electors shall vote *viva voce.* Electors for members to the General Council for 1828, shall be held at the places of holding the several courts and at the other two precincts in each District which are designated by this Convention were elected; and the District Judges shall superintend the elections within the precincts of their respective Court Houses, and the Marshals & Sheriffs shall superintend within the precincts which may be assigned them by the Circuit Judges of their respective Districts, together with one other person, who shall be appointed by the Circuit Judges for each precinct within their respective Districts; and the Circuit Judges shall also appoint a clerk to each precinct.—The superintendents and clerks shall, on the Wednesday morning succeeding the election, assemble at their respective Court Houses and proceed to examine and ascertain the true state of the polls, and shall issue to each member, duly elected, a certificate; and also make an official return of the state of the polls of election to the principal Chief, and it shall be the du-

[Cherokee syllabary columns]

46

translation of part of the gospel of St. John was made by a young Cherokee convert, John Arch, in 1824, and copied hundreds of times; printed Cherokee Bibles soon followed. On the other hand, it enabled the keepers of traditional Cherokee lore to record their ritual formulas and secret knowledge in a way untainted by white civilization and hidden from white eyes.

Most important, Sequoyah's invention gave every Cherokee a voice in the affairs of the nation. The first issue of their national newspaper, the bilingual *Cherokee Phoenix* (later the *Cherokee Advocate*), appeared on February 21, 1828, under the editorship of John Ridge's cousin Elias Boudinot. From the beginning, it was a powerful and controversial debating floor for the Cherokees at a time of rapid and radical change.

In the *Cherokee Phoenix* Elias Boudinot argued the Cherokee cause eloquently and with passion. The nub of the matter had already been stated in John Ridge's letter of 1827: "It is true we Govern ourselves, but yet we live in fear. We are urged by these strangers to make room for their settlements & go farther west."

The Cherokee envisaged the world as a great island floating in a sea of water, suspended at the north, south, east, and west by a cord hanging down from the sky vault, which was made of solid rock. When the world grows old and worn out, they believed, the cords will break and let the earth sink down beneath the ocean. All will be water again, as it was in the beginning.

The animal-people who existed at the beginning in the world above this one were too crowded and needed more room. So they sent the little water-beetle, "Beaver's Grandchild," to look for more land. The water-beetle brought up mud from the bottom of the primal ocean and with it made the earth.

Then the animal-people sent the Great Buzzard to

The front page of the first issue of the *Cherokee Phoenix* 1828

Because Sequoyah's syllabary needed eighty-six characters, as opposed to the twenty-six in the English alphabet, type for it had to be specially cast in Boston before it could be used in printing. The first printed use was for a translation of the first five verses of Genesis, followed closely by the first number of the Cherokee Phoenix, *which was published in both Cherokee and English; the front page of the first issue printed the Constitution of the Cherokee Nation. In 1835 the paper was closed down by the Georgia authorities.*

A Winnebago dance pouch made from the skin of an otter
19th century

A Cherokee myth tells how in the Creation time the Rabbit stole the Otter's coat. On the way to a council of the animals to decide who had the finest coat, the Rabbit and the Otter slept beside the river. The Rabbit threw hot coals in the air, tricking the Otter into thinking it was raining fire; so the Otter jumped into the river, and the Rabbit took the Otter's coat.

prepare the earth for habitation, for it was still too soft and wet. He flew all over the new land. By the time he reached the Cherokee country, he was very tired. His flapping wings began to touch the ground, and wherever they struck the earth they made a valley, and wherever they went up again they raised a mountain.

This ancestral Cherokee country, a fertile land with high wooded mountains and deep rich valleys, had been under threat since the moment the first white man laid eyes on it. Gradually, in one shoddy treaty after another, it had been appropriated by the whites. By 1823 the Cherokee had reached the end of that road. Their principal leaders—Pathkiller, Charles Hicks, Major Ridge, and John Ross—told the federal commissioners who were lobbying hard for further land concessions, "It is the fixed and unalterable determination of this nation never again to cede one foot more of land."

But it was not just a matter of land. There was also the discovery, about 1828, of gold on Ward's Creek, a western branch of the Chestatee River in Georgia, in the heart of the Cherokee country. And there was the election to the office of president of the United States, in November 1828, of Andrew Jackson, a frontiersman who had made his name fighting, not aiding, the Indians. It was Jackson who, with Cherokee help, had destroyed the Creek at Horseshoe Bend.

All the splendid new buildings that the Cherokee could erect, all the fine-sounding constitutions and laws they could enact, paled into insignificance for the white man beside the primitive lure of gold. And all the improvements the Cherokee could make to their territory, turning wild country into productive farmland, failed to impress their white neighbors with their progress in "civilization." Instead, the Cherokee's work made the land look all the more attractive.

On December 20, 1828, the state of Georgia passed an act, to come into effect on June 1, 1830, annexing all Cherokee land in Georgia and brushing aside all Cherokee laws and customs. Furthermore, "No Indian or descendant of any Indian residing within the Creek or Cherokee nations of Indians, shall be deemed a competent witness in any court of this State to which a white person may be a party."

Before long, all the Cherokee lands in Georgia (home to about half of the eastern Cherokee, and source of most of the Cherokee's wealth) had been surveyed and divided into "land lots" and "gold lots" to be apportioned among the white citizens of Georgia by lottery. Every white citizen received a ticket. It was an exciting time, and a new popular song caught the mood exactly:

> All I ask in this creation
> Is a pretty little wife and a big plantation
> Way up yonder in the Cherokee Nation.

The Cherokee themselves vigorously asserted their rights, both through their principal chief, John Ross, and through the editorials of Elias Boudinot in the *Cherokee Phoenix*. Some whites saw the justice of the Indians' case. One was Jeremiah Evarts, the chief administrative officer of the American Board of Commissioners for Foreign Missions, a consortium of missionary bodies.

In the latter half of 1829 Evarts published twenty-four "Essays on the Present Crisis in the Condition of the American Indians," under the pseudonym William Penn. Everts painstakingly outlined the legal and human rights of the Cherokee and the legal and moral obligations of the U.S. government. In a summary of the essays sent to congressmen, his first argument was simple and to the point: "The American Indians, now living upon lands derived from their ancestors, and never alienated nor surrendered, have a perfect right to the continued and undisturbed

possession of these lands." The forced removal of the Cherokee from their ancestral lands would be, Evarts argued, "an instance of gross and cruel oppression."

The Cherokee could also speak eloquently for themselves. John Ridge impressed many with his fluent, unaffected oratory. His polished delivery and educated manner were one more proof of how "civilized" the Cherokee had become. He told an audience in Philadelphia:

> You asked us to throw off the hunter and warrior state: We did so—you asked us to form a republican government: We did so—adopting your own as a model. You asked us to cultivate the earth, and learn the mechanic arts: We did so. You asked us to learn to read: We did so. You asked us to cast away our idols, and worship your God: We did so.

But these claims of civilization could not convince the majority. They shared the view of Lewis Cass, governor of Michigan Territory, who argued, in an influential counterblast to Evarts, that the Cherokee were an "ignorant and barbarous" people who were standing in the way of progress. Senator John Forsyth of Georgia grudgingly allowed that the Indians were "somewhat like human beings," but he argued strongly that this did not mean that they were entitled, or ever would be entitled, to equal civil and political rights.

After a bitter debate, the Indian Removal Act was signed into law by President Andrew Jackson on May 28, 1830. He declared, "It gives me pleasure to announce to Congress that the benevolent policy of the Government, steadily pursued for nearly thirty years, in relation to the removal of the Indians beyond the white settlements is approaching a happy consummation."

It was at this point that the Cherokee leadership split into two factions. The principal chief, John Ross, remained utterly opposed to removal and determined not to allow it

James Mooney
Cherokees Katalsta and her daughter Ewi-Katalsta making traditional pottery on Qualla Reservation, North Carolina 1888

Mooney regarded Katalsta as the last traditional Cherokee potter. She was the daughter of Yonaguska, the peace chief of the eastern Cherokee. He was also a prophet who visited the spirit world in a trance and talked with God, as a consquence of which his entire people signed a pledge not to drink whiskey. Yonaguska was very mistrustful of missionaries. He was once brought a copy of the Bible translated into Cherokee. He listened to a few chapters, and remarked, "Well, it seems to be a good book— strange that the white people are not better, after having had it so long."

after Charles Bird King
David Vann 1835–36

David Vann was a prominent mixed-blood chief who believed that the way forward for the Cherokee lay through education. He was among those who voted the money to set up the Cherokee Phoenix, *and he was a trusted emissary of Major Ridge, undertaking various complex and sensitive negotiations in Washington.*

to happen. John Ridge and Elias Boudinot, on the other hand, understood that removal was now inevitable and resolved to negotiate for the best deal they could get. Boudinot's brother Stand Watie and John Ridge's father, Major Ridge, stood beside them, forming what is known as the Treaty Party.

In October 1832 the first Georgia lotteries were held. The houses and land of both John Ridge and Major Ridge were allotted to new—white—owners, though they were allowed to remain in their homes while treaty negotiations were in progress. This favorable treatment allowed others to argue that the Treaty Party members were in it for their personal gain rather than the public good.

Certainly, most ordinary Cherokees were not so lucky. They found themselves dispossessed of their homes and their lands by people so certain of their right to do so that they scarcely even noticed they were doing it.

The Brandon family was typical. Down-on-his-luck John Brandon had been so determined to take advantage of this once-in-a-lifetime opportunity that he raised the money to buy thirteen tickets from other citizens, not one of which won anything. Undaunted, he sold yet more of his possessions and purchased from one of the lucky winners a plot of land in Cass County, on the Etowah River.

The Brandons' story was recorded by John's wife, Zillah Haynie Brandon, in her old age. She recalled how they moved to their new land in December 1835.

> The weather was excessively cold, but on the sixth day after our departure, we arrived at the place of our destination [and] found a family of *Indians occupying our house,* which, by the way, was a very poor one without floor or loft. The Indians set about moving out, though, with looks as magisterial as if they had been kings seated upon thrones in royal robes with a retinue about them,

leaning upon the sceptres. They would not deign to look at us, much less speak to us. That, though, was characteristic of that people: they are seldom known to speak to strangers, that is, among the white people. As soon, however, as they were out, we spread carpets over the dirt floor and unloaded the wagons and went in with thankful hearts.

When John Ross came home from Washington in 1833, having refused President Jackson's offer of new land in the west and compensation of three million dollars, he discovered his own house in the hands of a stranger.

Negotiations continued. President Jackson negotiated both with Ross, the acknowledged official leader of the Cherokee, and with various other factions, including Ross's brother, Andrew. Back home in the Cherokee Nation, the rivalries between these factions exploded into violent argument and even bloodshed. "Our Nation is crumbling into ruin," wrote John Ridge. As a result, John Ridge and Elias Boudinot resigned from the Cherokee Council and in 1835 led a delegation to Washington to agree on treaty terms with the War Department. The secretary of war was now Lewis Cass, the man who had argued so forcefully that the removal of the "ignorant and barbarous" Cherokee was nothing less than the will of God.

Alarmed by this development, John Ross approached Cass with a counterproposal: he would sell the Cherokee lands for twenty million dollars. With this sum (the true value, Ross felt, of the gold reserves beneath the Cherokee territory) he could purchase a new homeland for the Cherokee. He had his heart set on a new life in Mexico. When that proposal was rejected, Ross asked the Senate to decide a fair figure. They offered a mere five million—not enough for Ross to accept and save face.

So the War Department returned to its negotiations with the Ridge-Boudinot delegation. They offered them similar terms—four and a half million dollars for the Cherokee lands, thirteen million acres of land in the new Indian Territory in the west, and other benefits.

John Ridge returned home to try to convince the Cherokee Nation that the deal he had negotiated was the best they could achieve. He hoped to win over Ross and the traditionalists to this view, but the split between his party and John Ross was too wide. On December 29, 1835, at Elias Boudinot's house in New Echota, Georgia, twenty delegates of the Treaty Party signed the treaty. As Major Ridge made the X that signified his name, he said, "I have signed my death warrant."

Major Ridge took the signed treaty to Washington, where John Ridge and Stand Watie added their names to it. This New Echota Treaty was of doubtful legality, for it did not have the backing either of the principal chief, John Ross, or of the Cherokee Nation in general. Nevertheless it was ratified by the Senate.

Ross was furious. He would not, could not, accept what had happened. He was sure that somehow he could get the treaty annulled. The government, he said, was trying "to legislate the Indians off the land." Ross organized a petition of protest, filled with X's representing the signatures of sixteen thousand Cherokees (nearly the entire body of the eastern Cherokee), but this was brushed aside by the authorities. Chief Junaluska, one of the Cherokees who had fought for President Jackson in the Creek War, said, "If I had known that Jackson would drive us from our homes I would have killed him that day at the Horseshoe."

Major W. M. Davis was appointed to make a list of the Cherokees in preparation for removing them from their land. He wrote to Secretary of War Lewis Cass that the Treaty of New Echota was "no treaty at all," and warned,

"The Cherokee are a peaceable, harmless people, but you may drive them to desperation, and this treaty can not be carried into effect except by the strong arm of force."

General John Wool, who was in command of the troops sent to enforce the treaty, was no more enthusiastic about the work than Davis. He wrote to Cass, "The whole scene since I have been in this country has been nothing but a heart-rending one." Nevertheless, he did his duty and disarmed the Cherokee.

Right up to the end, the Cherokee had faith in Ross. They believed that justice would prevail, that they would remain in their homeland. When the time allowed for their departure expired, only two thousand out of seventeen thousand had gone west.

General Winfield Scott, commanding a force of some seven thousand men, was commissioned to oversee the removal of the Cherokee, by force if necessary. The Cherokee were rounded up at bayonet point and penned in stockades while the lawless white men who followed on the heels of the soldiers looted and pillaged their homes. Even the Indian graves were desecrated by treasure hunters looking for silver pendants buried with the dead. One Georgia volunteer with Scott's force, later a colonel in the Confederate army, summed up the scene: "I fought through the Civil War and have seen men shot to pieces and slaughtered by thousands, but the Cherokee removal was the cruelest work I ever knew."

Hundreds of Cherokees died of illness and malnutrition in the stockades, and many hundreds more on the terrible overland journey from Rattlesnake Springs in Tennessee to their new home in the Indian Territory. The journey took six months, from October 1838 to March 1839, in the bitter winter weather. Estimates vary as to how many succumbed to sickness and exposure on the way, but the figure is usually sct at four thousand—a quarter of the

after Charles Bird King
John Ross 1835–36

John Ross served the Cherokee people faithfully for fifty-seven years, the last forty of them as principal chief. He spent up to half of each year in Washington, lobbying for Cherokee rights and striving to protect Cherokee unity and sovereignty. Only one-eighth Cherokee by ancestry, he was nevertheless the chosen leader of the traditional Cherokees, the full-bloods, and they stayed loyal to him throughout the bitter trials of the day.

Feather wand of the Cherokee Eagle Dance 1900

This feather wand was made for the ethnologist James Mooney by John Ax (Itagunahi), a storyteller from whom Mooney recorded many Cherokee myths. The eagle is the great sacred bird of the Cherokee, and an eagle could be killed only by a professional eagle killer, who knew all the necessary prayers. Should any person dream of eagles or eagle feathers, they must arrange an Eagle Dance as soon as possible or someone in their family would die. So an eagle killer would be employed, and when the feathers were brought in, the dance was held that very night. A tail from a golden eagle was regarded as equivalent in value to a horse.

eastern Cherokee. Among the dead was Quatie Ross, the wife of John Ross.

The Cherokee call the journey "the Trail Where We Cried"—the Trail of Tears.

It was remembered in 1932 by Rebecca Neugin, then nearly a hundred years old. Rebecca was only three at the time of the removal. She told historian Grant Foreman:

> When the soldiers came to our house my father wanted to fight, but my mother told him that the soldiers would kill him if he did and we surrendered without a fight. They drove us out of our house to join other prisoners in a stockade. After they took us away my mother begged them to let her go back and get some bedding. So they let her go back and she brought what bedding and a few cooking utensils she could carry and had to leave behind all of our other household possessions. My father had a wagon pulled by two spans of oxen to haul us in. Eight of my brothers and sisters and two or three widow women and children rode with us. My brother Dick who was a good deal older than I was walked along with a long whip which he popped over the backs of the oxen and drove them all the way. My father and mother walked all the way also.

Many children died on the trail, of whooping cough and other diseases. Rebecca was one of the lucky ones.

Remarkably, there was only one case of armed resistance to the soldiers. The ringleader was the old medicine man Tsali, whose vision of the end of the world had led to the panic of 1812. Infuriated by the way soldiers prodded his elderly wife with their bayonets to move her along, Tsali said something in Cherokee to the other men being herded with them, and before the soldiers knew what was happening, the Cherokees had turned on them. Although the Cherokees were unarmed, surprise was on their side. They killed one soldier, and the rest fled. Tsali and his little band of renegades escaped to the mountains, to join a group of about a thousand diehards under the command of Utsala.

General Scott realized it was a hopeless task scouring the mountains for the resisters, especially as these Qualla Cherokees were living outside the tribal territory, on land bought for them by a friendly white man, and were therefore not included in the removal. So Scott offered to leave them alone so long as they surrendered Tsali. He, his brother, and his sons turned themselves in voluntarily; General Scott ordered a group of Cherokee prisoners to form the firing squad that shot them. Only Wasituna ("Washington"), Tsali's youngest son, was spared.

The mountain Cherokees left behind in North Carolina formed the eastern band of the nation, the most traditional and conservative of all the various factions into which the Cherokee had now split. Arriving in the Indian Territory, John Ross found the western band of Cherokees from Arkansas already established there and unwilling to let the new arrivals have everything their own way. The Ridge-Boudinot Treaty Party allied themselves with these western Cherokees, in opposition to Ross's authority.

The history of the Cherokee over the next few years was one of infighting, factionalism, and a general jostling for power and influence. On June 22, 1839, Major Ridge, John Ridge, and Elias Boudinot were all murdered by supporters of Ross, in accordance with a law of the Cherokee Nation that decreed death for anyone who ceded tribal lands without authority from the general council. The resentment against these men had risen so high that, after his murder, Boudinot's body was hacked to pieces.

Stand Watie, Boudinot's brother, escaped and swore vengeance against Ross, a vengeance he was to exact during the Civil War, when, as a Confederate general, he took pleasure in burning Ross's new house to the ground.

The Civil War found the Cherokee once more caught between two powerful opposing forces, as they had been between the French and the British and then between the

Anon.
The Cherokee payment *c.* 1894

The annual payment of monies and goods due under various treaties also served as a social occasion for those who came to claim what they were owed. Here several white men count out coins at a table, with a crowd of Cherokees gathered round.

British and the Americans. The Cherokee Nation was divided: Stand Watie and his supporters in the secret proslavery society known as the Knights of the Golden Circle supported the Confederate cause; John Ross and his supporters in the traditionalist Keetoowah Society (also known as the Pin Indians because of the insignia of crossed pins they wore on their coats) tried to remain neutral.

The war brought nothing but suffering to the Cherokee. Stand Watie threw in his lot completely with the Confederates and after the war demanded that the Cherokee Nation be divided in two. John Ross, meanwhile, had tried to keep both sides happy and, in doing so, made himself appear a traitor to both. The commissioners appointed to negotiate articles of peace with the tribes (including the Seneca Indian

Colonel Ely S. Parker) refused to recognize Ross as chief of the Cherokee. It seemed as if Stand Watie would get his way; he and his party even agreed and signed a treaty that, if ratified, would have split the Cherokee Nation down the middle.

In the end, however, Ross won the day. A new treaty was signed; the nation was not divided; John Ross remained principal chief of the Cherokee. The price he paid was high, not only in making further concessions of land but in allowing two railroad rights-of-way through the Cherokee territory.

Four days after this treaty was ratified by the U.S. Senate, John Ross died, aged seventy-seven.

His legacy was a nation that remained true to itself despite the fierce political and personal rivalries that so divided and weakened it in its time of need. Starting again from scratch, the Cherokee recaptured in the Indian Territory (now part of Oklahoma) much of the forward momentum that had characterized their society in the years before the removal. They built a fine new capital at Tahlequah, continued publishing newspapers and books in Cherokee and English, founded their own schools, and reestablished their legislature and their judicial system.

This independence was curtailed in 1898, when the Curtis Act abolished all tribal law and government, and again in 1907 when the state of Oklahoma was created. To hold land in common, as the Cherokee had always done, was declared "non-American." The Cherokees were forced to accept individual allotments of land, and many of them were cheated out of their due.

The logical end of this sorry tale would be to say that after this the Cherokee dwindled away and, by melting into the general populace, became culturally extinct. But the opposite is true. Today there are over 250,000 Cherokees. As a people, they have lost and suffered much, but they have endured and once more grown strong.

They are still the Aniyunwiya, the Principal People.

4 THIS IS OUR LAND

My people, we were born in this country; this is our land. God put our fathers and mothers here. We have lived here in peace. . . . Now, what shall I do? Shall I run every time I see white people? If I do, they will chase us from valley to mountain, and from mountain to valley, and kill us all.

Father of Captain Jack (Modoc)

When the English explorer Sir Francis Drake landed in California in 1579, he found the natives to be "people of a tractable, free, and loving nature, without guile or treachery." Far from being ferocious warriors, the hunter-gatherer tribes of California were distinguished by their gentleness. They lived in small bands, coming together in large groups only at the twice-yearly dances that ensured the renewal, and therefore continuance, of the world.

It is estimated that at the time of Columbus there were 700,000 Native Americans in California. By the mid-1840s there were only 200,000. White men's diseases carried off many, and the traditional life of the Indians was disrupted by the Spanish practice of forcing them into missions, where they were first baptized as Christians and then used as forced labor in the fields. Nevertheless, when Mexico ceded California to the United States in 1848, the Californian Indians were still living an approximation of their life before contact with Europeans. All of this was to change with horrible swiftness and brutality.

The crucial event was the discovery of gold at Sutter's Mill in 1848, which sparked the California gold rush. White settlers poured across the Rockies. These miners were for the most part crude, greedy men. They despised the

Edward Sheriff Curtis
White Deerskin Dance costume 1924

The Deerskin Dance of the Hupa was one of many Californian world-renewal rituals; it also served a social purpose and enabled the dancers to display their wealth in the form of elaborate dance costumes. In 1902 a Hupa woman named Nettie Miskût remembered her tribe's first contact with the whites when she was a child: "When they first came along with a pack-train we ran away and hid. . . . Those with brave hearts traded with them. Some of us ran away from them. The babies were hid in the storage baskets."

Indians, whom they derisively called "Diggers" because they lived partly on roots dug from the ground with sticks.

George Crook was a young lieutenant in the mining town of Yreka. Later, as a general, he recalled, "It was of no infrequent occurrence for an Indian to be shot down in cold blood, or a squaw to be raped by some brute. Such a thing as a white man being punished for outraging an Indian was unheard of."

Miners went on Indian hunts, killing any men they found and taking the women and children captive. Many of the women were forced into prostitution, while the children were sold as slaves or indentured laborers. One California newspaper of 1854 reported, "Abducting Indian children has become quite a common practice. Nearly all of the children belonging to some of the Indian tribes in the northern part of the state have been stolen. They are taken to the southern part of the state, and there sold." By 1870 there were only thirty-one thousand Native Americans in California, while the number of whites had risen a hundredfold to over half a million.

The story of the Yana is in essence the story of most Californian tribes. The Yana probably never numbered more than two thousand people in all, divided into four known groups—the Northern, Central, and Southern Yana, and the Yahi—each of which spoke its own dialect. Like so many Native American tribal names, the names Yana and Yahi both mean simply "People." They lived in the southern Cascade foothills in the upper Sacramento River valley. Neighboring peoples included the Wintu, Achumawi, Atsugewi, Maidu, and Nomlaki.

The Yana were hunter-gatherers. They lived on salmon from the rivers, game such as deer and rabbits, roots, tubers, bulbs, and the Californian staple, acorns. Yana life was organized at the village level. The Northern and Central Yana lived in multifamily dwellings, covered in

earth and entered through the smoke hole in the roof. The
Southern Yana and Yahi lived in single-family conical structures made of branches or bark.

The Yana believed that the first Yanas were created from
buckeye sticks by Jupka, the butterfly of the wild silkworm
(or, in another version, by Lizard and Cottontail Rabbit).
Jupka gave them their land to live in. "'You will eat clover,'
said he, 'and roots. I will give you sticks to dig these roots.

Saxton Pope
Ishi demonstrating a rabbit call 1914

Californian Indians almost never speak their own name. Ishi never revealed his private Yaha name to his white friends. He was given the name Ishi (meaning "man" in Yana) by Alfred L. Kroeber. Here he is shown demonstrating a Yahi technique for hunting rabbits. The Yana dressed simply: the wealthy men in buckskin leggings, the poorer ones like Ishi in a simple apron. The women wore a skirt of leather tassels braided with grass, or an apron of shredded bark or tules.

You will eat fish, too, and venison. Eat and be strong, be good Yana people.'"

Study of their language suggests that the Yana had been in northern California for at least three or four thousand years. Their simple existence remained undisturbed until first contact with whites in 1821. It was not until 1845 that the first white dwellings were constucted in Yana territory. By 1848 whites were regularly crossing Yana land on the California-Oregon trail.

The first massacre of Yanas occurred in 1846 at Bloody Island in the Sacramento River, where a peaceful gathering of Indians was attacked by Captain John Frémont. This set a grisly pattern, and in August 1864 almost all the remaining Yanas were slaughtered by white settlers.

The pretext for this massacre was the murder of two white women, Mrs. Allen and Mrs. Dirsch, by Indians living around Mill Creek, who may have been Yahis. In revenge, two parties of white men, under the leadership of Robert A. Anderson and Hiram Good, fell indiscriminately on the Yana. "They had resolved," writes Jeremiah Curtin, who made careful enquiries in 1895, "to exterminate the whole nation." Curtin's account makes grim reading.

> At Millville, twelve miles east of Redding, white men seized two Yana girls and a man. These they shot about fifty yards from the village hotel. At another place they came to the house of a white woman who had a Yana girl, seven or eight years of age. They seized this child, in spite of the woman, and shot her through the head. "We must kill them, big and little," said the leader; "nits will be lice."

By the time Anderson and Good had finished their work, it is estimated, only fifty Yanas remained alive.

In 1911 an exhausted, starving man was taken into custody in the northern California town of Oroville and then delivered into the care of the distinguished anthropologist Professor Alfred L. Kroeber. This man was Ishi, the sole living member of the Yahi people, "the last wild Indian in North America." The probable date of his birth was 1862; he had been in hiding in the hills all his life. Ishi spent four years and seven months as a kind of living museum piece in the University of California Museum of Anthropology before succumbing to tuberculosis. Kroeber said of him, "He was the most patient man I ever knew."

The gentle lifestyle of the Californian Indians was no match for the casual brutality of the whites who flooded into their territory during the gold rush. They offered no concerted resistance in defense of their lands and their way of life. Not all their stories were as tragic in their finality as that of the Yahi, but they followed a similar pattern.

Farther north, the nations of the Plateau (the region drained by the Columbia and Fraser rivers) were more inclined to fight back. The Modoc (a Californian tribe geographically but culturally aligned with the Plateau peoples) fought a desperate war of resistance among the desolate lava beds south of Tule Lake. Their leader was Kintpuash, known as Captain Jack.

In 1846 Lindsay and Jesse Applegate had opened a southern branch of the Oregon Trail through Modoc country. The Modoc war chief at the time, Old Schonchin, took to ambushing wagon trains along the Applegate trail, killing the men and taking the women and children as slaves. But in 1864 he was persuaded to sign a treaty of cession with the United States and lead his people onto a joint reservation with the Klamath. In mellow old age he explained his motivation.

> I thought if we killed all the white men we saw, that no more would come. We killed all we could, but they came, more and more, like the new grass in the spring. I looked around and saw that many of the young men were dead and could not come back to fight. My heart was sick. I threw down my gun. I said, "I will not fight again." I made friends with the white man.

At the time of signing the treaty, the Modoc believed that an earlier agreement, under which they would retain the land around Tule Lake, would still stand. Instead, they found themselves living as unwelcome strangers with their neighbors and rivals, the Klamath, on the Yainax reservation in the Klamath heartlands. In 1869, unable to bear the second-class status they endured in this unhappy situation, a party of Modocs under the leadership of Captain Jack returned to Tule Lake. And so the stage was set for a bitter and bloody confrontation.

Eadweard Muybridge
Modoc women and white men 1873

Tobey Riddle (Winema) is shown standing at the back of this group, with her husband, Frank Riddle, to her right and Captain Oliver C. Applegate, the Indian agent at Yainax, to her left. The four Modoc women in front of them, prisoners in Applegate's charge, were (from the left) Laceles, blind Mehunolush, Saukaadush, and Lauwlauwwaush. Tobey and Frank Riddle's son Jeff tried to correct the errors of white historians in his own Indian History of the Modoc War.

The vivid nicknames by which they were known to the whites make Captain Jack's band sound like a crew of bloodthirsty pirates: Scarfaced Charley, Hooker Jim, Curley Headed Doctor, Black Jim, Humpy Joe, Schonchin John, Shacknasty Jim, Bogus Charley, Boston Charley, One-Eyed Mose, and Ellen's Man were among Jack's fifty-two warriors. Even Captain Jack's sister had a suitably grand title: Queen Mary. These names were bestowed on the Modocs by the miners at nearby Yreka; their real names were not so colorful. Queen Mary's Modoc name, Koalaka, means "hard-working woman."

The fact that the white settlers knew the Modocs well enough to give them all English names suggests that contact between the two groups was frequent and relatively friendly. Many of the settlers, known as "squaw men," lived with Modoc women. A typical case was that of

Frank Riddle, a prospector who bought a twelve-year-old Modoc girl, Winema (known as Tobey), from her father, Captain Jack's uncle, for the sum of two horses. Frank knew Winema was the girl for him because when he thought of her, he felt, as he put it, "a goneness in my heart." They lived happily together, eventually marrying, and each played a crucial part in the drama of the Modoc War, the only participants in the drama able to fully understand the viewpoints of both sides.

Yet behind these friendly relations lay a history of mutual distrust. The whites remembered the Modoc attacks on peaceful wagon trains. The Modoc remembered the night in 1852 when settler Ben Wright invited forty-six Modocs to a peace conference—at which he first attempted to poison them with strychnine and then opened fire, killing all except five. Captain Jack's father was the first to die.

One of the five who escaped was Schonchin John, brother of Old Schonchin, the headman of the reservation Modocs. But, unlike his brother, Schonchin John was not inclined to trust the whites. He remembered Ben Wright's treachery too clearly for that. As one white trader recalled, he "would get very excited talking about it."

Captain Jack, despite his defiance of the reservation treaty, was not interested in conflict with the whites. All he wanted was to live in his native country by Tule Lake, the land around which, in Modoc belief, the rest of the world had gradually been woven, like a traditional basket made from tule rushes. He said, "I don't know any other country. God gave me this country. He put my people here first. I was born here. My father was born here. I want to live here. I do not want to leave the ground where I was born."

Schonchin John's motivation was more complex, shaped both by resentment of white treachery and by rivalry with Captain Jack. In opposition to Jack, Schonchin John became the leader of the war party among the Modocs. He was supported in his angry talk not only by influential warriors such as Hooker Jim and Black Jim (Captain Jack's half brother), but also by the medicine man, Curley Headed Doctor.

Curley Headed Doctor was aflame with a new doctrine that in 1870 swept through the nations of the Plateau and the Great Basin (the area between the Sierra Nevada and the Rocky Mountains): the Ghost Dance. This was a movement of Native American revitalization, based on the vision of a Paiute (Numa) shaman named Wodziwob. Wodziwob promised that if the Indians danced and believed, the whites would be swept from the land and the Indian dead would return to life. The world would, in effect, come to an end and begin again, cleansed and renewed.

A botched attempt to arrest Captain Jack in November 1872 resulted in the death of one Modoc man and several women and children. Hooker Jim and Curley Headed Doctor led a revenge party, killing fourteen male settlers. Captain Jack, horrified, had to choose either to turn the culprits in or to fight. He counseled surrender.

> We have made a mistake. We cannot stand against the white men. Suppose we kill all these soldiers. More will come, and still more, and finally all the Modocs will be killed. . . . We must make the best terms we can. I do not want to fight the white man. I want no war. I want peace.

But Curley Headed Doctor was more persuasive. "I want war," he said, and he promised that he could use his powers to turn the white men's bullets away from the Modocs.

That night they danced the Ghost Dance. Curley Headed Doctor visited the spirit realm, to strengthen and renew his powers. In the morning, Curley Headed Doctor promised, he would raise a fog so intense it would utterly confuse the attacking Americans.

Captain Jack and his fifty-two warriors, with their women and children, had taken refuge in the Lava Beds, an unrelenting rocky landscape that looked, according to one

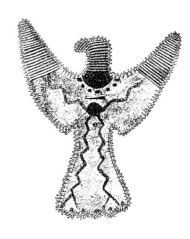

The Thunderbird
c. 1892

Belief in the Thunderbird, a vast bird whose shadow is the thunder cloud, whose flapping wings cause the thunderclaps, and whose flashing eyes send forth the lightning, is widespread (although not universal) among Native American peoples. Ghost Dancers often wore on their heads a small figure of the Thunderbird, like the one shown above, cut from rawhide and ornamented with beads. The zigzag lines coming from the Thunderbird's heart represent the lightning.

Louis Herman Heller
Curley Headed Doctor 1873

The Modoc medicine man Curley Headed Doctor provided the spiritual fuel for the Modoc War, leading Captain Jack's band in the circular Ghost Dance in which they sang songs such as this one recorded from the Paiutes:

> *Fog! Fog!*
> *Lightning! Lightning!*
> *Whirlwind! Whirlwind!*

Curley Headed Doctor lost faith in the protective powers of the Ghost Dance after Ellen's Man was killed. Because he surrendered with Hooker Jim, he was pardoned for his part in the hostilities.

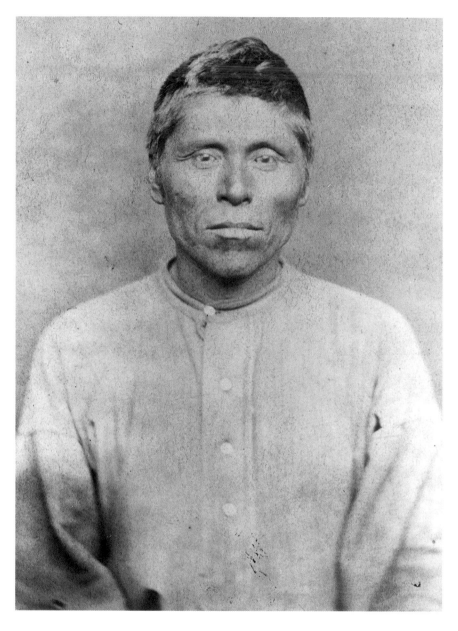

soldier, like "a black ocean tumbled into a thousand fantastic shapes, a wild chaos of ruin, desolation, and barrenness." The caves and ravines of the Lava Beds were easy to hide in, especially as the Modocs had a supply of cattle and knew the terrain. The four hundred soldiers sent to subdue Captain Jack were also thrown off balance on the morning of January 17, 1873, by a fog so thick that, as they marched into the Lava Beds, they disappeared from view.

By the end of the day the troops were retreating in panic and disarray. The Americans had lost thirty-seven men dead or seriously wounded, without inflicting any harm on the Modocs. Curley Headed Doctor's medicine had worked: First he brought a fog to confuse the enemy, and then he turned the white men's bullets so that no Modoc was hurt. "We can kill all the white men that come," he crowed.

The American troops were as demoralized as the Modocs were exuberant. One of their commanders, Captain R. F. Bernard, reported that many of the troops would rather serve twenty years imprisoned on Alcatraz Island for desertion than attack the enemy again in the Lava Beds.

Washington sent a peace commission, led by Albert B. Meacham, to try to settle the problem. In 1845, aged nineteen, Meacham had assisted in removing the Sac and Fox Indians to their reservation after the Black Hawk War. His approach to the Modoc was sympathetic, perhaps influenced by R. F. Bernard's further words in his report:

> This tribe was living in peace, subsisting themselves without the aid of anyone, when the attempt was made to force them to leave their native place, and to go and live amongst a people that have always been their bitterest enemies and who are now employed in the field against them. Men that would not fight under such circumstances are not worthy of life or liberty.

The Modocs were offered an amnesty—but only if they agreed to be removed from their lands. They could not keep even the desolate Lava Beds, although as Captain Jack wrily observed, "Nobody will ever want these rocks."

"I do not want to fight," Captain Jack told Meacham. But he added, "I am a Modoc. I am not afraid to die."

Meacham believed that Captain Jack was sincere in wanting peace and sent Captain Jack's cousin Tobey Riddle, who had been acting as an interpreter, to offer protection if he would surrender. The Modocs voted on the proposal. Eleven of them, including Captain Jack himself, wanted to accept it. But the others said no.

When Tobey rode out of the camp, a voice whispered to her, "Tell Old Man Meacham and all the men not to come to the council tent again—they get killed."

Captain Jack was firmly against the plan to murder the peace commissioners. He pleaded with the Modoc warriors not to consider it. He believed that if he only held firm in the negotiations, he could win them both the promised amnesty and an acceptable home. But the warriors mocked him, dressing him in a woman's hat and shawl, and deriding him as a coward and a squaw.

It was this accusation of cowardice that made Captain Jack agree to a plan that he knew would bring both shame and terrible retribution upon his people.

On April 11, 1873, Alfred Meacham wrote to his wife, "You may be a widow tonight." Then he and the other peace commissioners rode to the council tent unarmed as agreed, though Tobey Riddle had warned them clearly that if they went unarmed, they would certainly be killed. Captain Jack shot the army commander General Edward Canby, and then slit his throat. Boston Charley killed the Reverend Eleazer Thomas. Shacknasty Jim shot Meacham several times. Boston Charley was in the act of taking Meacham's balding scalp when the others retreated, and he scrambled to join them, leaving Tobey Riddle cradling Meacham's head in her lap. Amazingly, Meacham survived and still had a part to play in the Modoc tragedy.

The Modocs were jubilant, and certain that Curley Headed Doctor's medicine was strong enough to protect them. Right until the moment when an American cannonball landed in the central fire of the Modoc stronghold, they believed that he would be able to turn away the enemy's weapons.

Now the Modocs put their faith in the leadership of

Captain Jack. He knew they were all destined to die, but the Lava Beds were as good a place as any to make a last stand. Even now, with a thousand soldiers ranged against him, Captain Jack was able not just to hold the American troops at bay but to harry them at will. Of one patrol of sixty-six soldiers, twenty-seven were killed and seventeen wounded. The Modocs lost just one man, shot to death while plundering the battlefield.

Colonel Jefferson C. Davis was appointed to take over

the command. Davis took the time to regroup his troops and try to restore their morale. Delay was the best tactic he could have chosen, for Captain Jack and his band were running out of food and water. All they had to eat was whatever they could steal from the Americans.

In a skirmish near Sorass Lake the American troops managed for the first time to hold their own against a Modoc attack. The Modocs seized no new supplies, and even lost some of what they had. One of the Modoc warriors, Ellen's Man, was killed. The downhearted Modocs blamed Captain Jack for their troubles, and a dozen men and their families split off from his camp.

Among those who split with Hooker Jim were Bogus Charley, Curley Headed Doctor, and Shacknasty Jim. On May 22 they surrendered—twelve warriors and a raggle-taggle following described by an eyewitness as "half-naked children, aged squaws who could scarcely hobble, blind, lame, halt, bony." Hoping to ingratiate themselves with the Americans, they offered to bring in Captain Jack.

Hooker Jim and Bogus Charley led the soldiers to the canyon in which Captain Jack was holed up with his twenty-four remaining warriors. Group by group, the Modocs surrendered—first the women and children, then a number of warriors, including Scarfaced Charley and Schonchin John, and finally Captain Jack and his family.

Captain Jack and Schonchin John were placed in leg shackles to make sure they could not escape and confined to cells. Captain Jack, Schonchin John, Black Jim, Boston Charley, and two Modoc boys, Slolux and Barncho, were put on trial in Klamath Fort, Oregon. Those who had betrayed Captain Jack at the end were pardoned.

As the trial proceeded, the prisoners received an unexpected visitor. It was Alfred B. Meacham, still recovering from his wounds but flesh and blood and not a ghost, as Schonchin John ascertained by squeezing his arm. Captain

Ilka Hartmann
Pit River Protest
1979–80

This San Francisco demonstration for land rights was organized by Bill Wahpepah, a San Francisco Bay Area AIM leader. He was co-founder of the International Indian Treaty Council, which lobbies the United Nations for Indian rights.

Jack pleaded with Meacham to speak for him at the trial, for the Modocs had no legal counsel. But Meacham was not well enough to do it. And when the six were found guilty and sentenced to be hanged (although the two boys were reprieved), it was to Meacham that Captain Jack turned with his biggest worry. Death by hanging would trap his soul within his body; his spirit would never be free to dance and sing in the great house in the west to which the Modoc go when they die. But as Meacham's memoirs show, he did not understand what he was being told. The sentence was just, he said.

Perhaps the last words belong with Kintpuash—Captain Jack—as he tried to explain to the court what had led him to this point.

> I am on the edge of my grave; my life is in your people's hands. I charge the white people of wholesale murder. Not only once but many times. Think about Ben Wright. What did he do? He killed nearly fifty of my people. Among the killed was my own father. He was holding a peace council with them. Was he or any of his men punished? No, not one. Mind you, Ben Wright and his men were civilized white people. . . . Now here I am. Killed one man, after I had been fooled by him many times and forced to do the act by my own warriors. The law says, hang him. He is nothing but an Indian, anyhow. . . . So now I do quit talking. In a few days I will be no more. I now bid the world farewell.

5 THEY HAVE THEIR EYES ON THIS LAND

My ancestors were glad to see the white strangers come. My people made no trouble. Never thought about making trouble. . . . Only when they want to put us in one small place, taking us from our home country, trouble started.

Hemene Moxmox (Yellow Wolf), Nez Perce

For the whole of recorded history, the Nez Perce have lived in the Columbia Basin—in central Idaho and adjoining parts of Oregon and Washington. They lived by hunting game such as elk, deer, and mountain sheep, fishing for salmon and other fish in the Snake and Columbia rivers, and harvesting wild foods such as roots and berries.

Their name for themselves is Nimi'ipuu ("the People"), but early they acquired the French name Nez Percé ("Pierced Nose"), now commonly spelled, and pronounced, Nez Perce; before the nineteenth century they wore dentalium-shell ornaments from a piercing in the nasal septum. In language and culture they were similar to other Sahaptian-speaking nations of the southern Plateau, such as the Walla Walla, Yakama, and Umatilla peoples, although after they acquired horses around 1700, they frequently ventured into the Montana plains to hunt buffalo and to trade. The Nez Perce soon became famous breeders of horses, maintaining large herds.

The Nez Perce joined together for the great salmon runs in the spring and fall. Socially, they divided into villages, each with its own headman and village council; each village was formed into a number of bands, each with its

Leander Moorhouse
Hoosis Moxmox, Umatilla chief 1900

The Nez Perce and Umatilla were closely allied, with a similar Plateau culture and related Sahaptian languages. In 1855 the Umatilla, Cayuse, and Walla Walla agreed by treaty to live on the Umatilla Reservation in Oregon; it was suggested at one point that the Nez Perce should join them there.

own traditional territory and its own chief. There was no overall tribal chief, and even the band chiefs were spokesmen rather than rulers. It was a society in which bands, families, and individuals had a great deal of independence and freedom, but which was held together by shared values and mutual needs.

In adolescence, Nez Perce boys and girls would go out individually to sacred places on vision quests, hoping to acquire power from a wyakin, or guardian spirit. A wyakin might be an animal such as a grizzly bear, a natural phenomenon such as lightning, or a supernatural being such as a ghost. Power was invoked through special songs that were learned from the wyakin during the vision quest and sung at the important annual spirit dance in late winter. Such power might give luck in hunting or in warfare, or the ability to cure, to foretell the future, or to control the weather; it could also be used maliciously to cause sickness or misfortune.

Above such spirit powers the Nez Perce recognized a supreme creator, Hunyawat (often referred to as the Great Spirit Chief when Nez Perce tried to explain their religious concepts to the whites), who had made Mother Earth for them to live in. Hunyawat could be contacted by inspired individuals in the round dance of the Dreamer religion, founded by the Wanapam prophet Smohalla after a vision in 1860. Smohalla's cult spread from Washington Territory all over the Plateau; like many Native American religious movements, it foretold the coming destruction of the world, when the dead would be brought back to life.

Nez Perce individuals with power could be granted visions of the future, and it is said that one such vision predicted the coming of the whites. In 1805 this vision was fulfilled with the arrival of Meriwether Lewis and William Clark, leading the first white overland expedition to the Pacific Ocean. At this date there were approximately six thousand Nez Perces. They welcomed Lewis and Clark, gave them assistance, and in return received gifts and promises of friendship. Shortly afterward, the fur trade brought new prosperity to the Nez Perce, who supplied beaver pelts to the North West Company post on the upper Columbia. These initial contacts with the whites were all mutually beneficial.

Soon the Nez Perces became intrigued by Christianity, and excited by the concept of reading and writing. They were particularly curious about the special book that was apparently the source of the white man's power. In 1831 a delegation of Nez Perces retraced Lewis and Clark's tracks to St. Louis, where they were greeted by William Clark himself. Despite language difficulties, they managed to make it clear that their peoples would like instruction in the Christian religion.

Two Presbyterian missionaries, Samuel Parker and Marcus Whitman, were dispatched. Whitman settled with the Cayuse, while Parker found himself escorted all over the northwest by the Nez Perce, conducting religious services wherever they went. Parker was greatly struck by the Nez Perce, writing that they were "kind to strangers, and remarkably so to each other . . . they are scrupulously honest in all their dealings and lying is scarcely known."

By the next year the Nez Perce had a missionary to themselves, Henry H. Spalding. He was a moody and severe man, ill suited to his task. Like many such missionaries, he was interested only in imposing his own brand of Christianity on the Indians, and he made no effort to understand or to value their culture. He tried to outlaw traditional customs such as the popular stick game, used for gambling, and the round dance, with its drumming, dancing, and singing. More drastically, he wanted to replace the relatively easygoing social structures of the Nez Perce, which were based on equality, respect, and

Leander Moorhouse
Nez Perce warriors
1906

*These Nez Perce
warriors are merely
posing for the camera of
the enthusiastic amateur
photographer Major
Leander (Lee)
Moorhouse, the Indian
agent for Umatilla
County, but they give an
idea of the impressive
confidence of the
warriors of Chief
Joseph's day.*

community pressure, with "civilized" ones based on authority, law, and punishment.

Many Nez Perces were attracted by the spiritual side of Christianity, but they saw it as complementing their age-old beliefs and practices rather than replacing them. A shaman called Thunder Eyes told Spalding angrily that "he had received the wyakin when young, and could not throw it away." Learning to read and write, learning to farm, learning about the promises and ideals of the white man's religion—all these things were welcomed as positive benefits by the Nez Perce. But other elements of the new teaching—for instance, Henry Spalding's grim-faced use of a whip to chastise those, even warriors and chiefs, whom he judged mischievous or insolent—were alien and degrading to Nez Perce culture. Nevertheless, Spalding made a few converts. One of the most important was Tuekakas, principal chief of the Wallowa band, who was baptized Joseph.

In 1840 the Oregon Trail opened the northwest to wagon trains. A stream of white settlers brought increasing opportunities for trade—and less welcome gifts, including diseases like smallpox, measles, and scarlet fever, against which they had no immunity.

With the early wagons came a Delaware Indian from Kansas named Tom Hill. He married a Nez Perce girl and became devoted to his adopted tribe's religion and customs. Arguing from the experience of the Delawares, he told the Nez Perces bluntly that the missionaries should be driven out.

The Nez Perces began to turn their backs on Spalding. In 1842, 225 pupils—half of them adults—were enrolled in the mission school, but gradually they stopped attending, and in 1846 the school closed.

A similar reaction against missionaries was gathering momentum elsewhere. In 1847 the Cayuses, fired up by a rumor that a measles epidemic was the result of Marcus Whitman's deliberately poisoning them in order to steal their land, attacked the mission at Waiilatpu, killing the Whitmans and eleven others. As a result, Spalding abandoned his mission to the Nez Perce at Lapwai, Idaho. The hope expressed by fellow missionary Elkanah Walker that "the influence of the gospel will have the tendency to make them more submissive to the rule of the whites" had perished.

In the spring of 1849 a territorial government was established over the Oregon country, which was then split into two parts, Oregon and Washington, along an east-west line. Chief Kamiakin of the Yakama (Yakima) tried to unite all the nations of the Columbia Basin to resist, but to no avail. In May 1855 they were summoned by the governor of the Washington Territory, Isaac Stevens, to a council in the Walla Walla Valley. Five thousand Indians attended this council, at which they were reassured by Superintendent of Indian Affairs Joel Palmer, "If we make a treaty with you . . . you can rely on all its provisions being carried out strictly."

Tauitau, a Cayuse chief, put the Indians' main objection into words. "I hear what this earth says," he declared. "The earth says, God has placed me here." But his words were swept aside, and treaties were agreed that would remove the various Plateau nations from their land and herd them into two reservations: a predominantly Yakama one in Washington and a predominantly Umatilla one in Oregon.

Just as the council was about to break up, an aged Nez Perce war chief named Apash Wyakaikt—an ally of Kamiakin's—returned from a buffalo-hunting trip to the plains. He arrived with three other elderly warriors, all painted for war. "My people," he cried, "what have you done? While I was gone, you have sold my country. I have come home, and there is not a place on which to pitch my lodge."

The Nez Perces impressed the whites with their note taking at meetings and with their beautifully conducted Sunday services. Under the leadership of a chief named Lawyer, whose wish for his nation was "peace, plows, and schools," they negotiated a separate deal. They gave up some of their outer territory in return for $200,000 in goods and government aid to build schools, a hospital, mills, and a blacksmith's shop.

Almost immediately, white settlers flooded into the Indians' land, and the dispossessed tribes responded by killing as many of them as they could. The whole region erupted in what is known, because of Chief Kamiakin's leadership, as the Yakima War—a conflict as doomed as the similar Modoc War, which was taking place at the same time and for the same reasons in southwest Oregon and northern California.

During this period of conflict the Nez Perce, true to the treaty they had signed, remained neutral. Kamiakin's Nez Perce friends and allies, such as Apash Wyakaikt, stayed at home; some of Lawyer's supporters even felt obliged to enlist in the Washington Territorial Volunteers to support the white men against the "hostiles."

The Nez Perces seemed for a while to have reached an accommodation with the whites, which would protect them from unwanted interference and allow them to live a relatively independent life on their ancestral lands. But all that was to change in 1861, when a gold rush brought a flood of new settlers into Oregon. Many of the whites chose to make their new homes in the very heart of the Nez Perce reservation.

The Nez Perce were already divided into pro- and antitreaty parties; the influx of new settlers intensified this division. The very fabric of Nez Perce society began to disintegrate, as hard liquor and money flowed through the reservation. One miner wrote, "What a miracle rum has wrought. What Christianity and civilization could not accomplish in decades, liquor has accomplished in a few short months."

Some traditionalists wanted to join forces with the Shoshone to drive the white men from the land. But even some of those who had been vehemently opposed to the treaty could not resist joining in the gold rush spoils. Koolkool Snehee (Red Owl), a chief who had been a noted buffalo hunter, said:

> The white men dig up and take the gold; what then? *We* get some of it. They buy our beef and pay for it with some of this gold. Our buffalo robes they exchange for gold or blankets. I am an Indian, and don't know how to farm; but I am going to learn. . . . They will buy my corn and other things that I shall grow on my farm. No! I have so far been for war, but now my eyes are open. I say peace.

By 1862 there were 18,960 whites living on the Nez Perce reservation, from which whites were supposed to be strictly excluded by the 1854 treaty. The government's response to this was to negotiate a new treaty with Lawyer, whom they regarded as the head chief of all the Nez Perce.

Anon.
Chief Joseph *c.* 1877

Chief Joseph is seen here much as he looked during his negotiations with General Howard, and the subsequent Nez Perce War, sometimes called Chief Joseph's War.

The new reservation was less than 10 percent of the area of the old one. Most of the Nez Perce land, including the lush and beautiful Wallowa Valley, had been sold for a promised price of less than eight cents an acre.

Spalding's prize convert, Joseph, chief of the Wallowa band, was disgusted. He tore up his Bible and became once more Tuekakas.

In 1871 Tuekakas died. On his deathbed he told his son Hinmahtooyahlatkekht:

> You are the chief of these people. They look to you to guide them. Always remember that your father never sold his country. You must stop your ears whenever you are asked to sign a treaty selling your home. A few years

more, and white men will be all around you. They have their eyes on this land. My son, never forget my dying words. This country holds your father's body. Never sell the bones of your father and your mother.

Hinmahtooyahlatkekht—better known by the English name Chief Joseph—took these words to heart. He refused to abandon the Wallowa, "that beautiful valley of winding waters." He even managed to get President Ulysses S. Grant to declare it a reservation.

But only two years later, under pressure from white settlers, the president changed his mind. Chief Joseph and his band had to go. General Oliver Otis Howard was sent to negotiate their removal to a reservation in Idaho. When Chief Joseph went to see the general at Fort Lapwai, he took with him a Nez Perce Dreamer prophet named Toohoolhoolzote.

No one could have been more irritating to the practical-minded General Howard than Toohoolhoolzote. The conversation went round and round in circles until the general snapped: "Twenty times over you repeat that the earth is your mother and about chieftainship from the earth. Let us hear it no more, but come to business at once."

Toohoolhoolzote was unimpressed by such bluster. "Who can tell me what I must do in my own country?" he asked. The exasperated general had him arrested, as the only effective means of silencing him. More than anything else, the discourtesy of this act—the imprisonment of an invited guest—ensured that the removal of Chief Joseph's people would not be peaceful.

The Nez Perces were proud to claim—not strictly accurately—that up to this point no Nez Perce had ever killed a white man. Now Chief Joseph was given just thirty days to take his people to join the rest of the Nez Perces on the reservation in Idaho; refusal to go would be regarded as an act of war.

With a heavy heart, Chief Joseph prepared to do as he was told. But some of the young warriors were so angry, they could not be restrained. They set off on a killing spree that left twenty white men dead—and Chief Joseph and his people at war with the United States of America.

Chief Joseph himself was a civil chief, not a war chief; as was the Nez Perce custom, he spoke only for his own band of people. His Wallowa band was allied in rebellion with those of four other chiefs: White Bird, Looking Glass, Toohoolhoolzote, and Husishusis Kute. It was Looking Glass, the son of old Apash Wyakaikt, who was elected the group's war chief.

Together, the bands numbered about 250 warriors. The total population of around 700 included women, children, and the sick and elderly. In addition, they were burdened by a herd of three thousand ponies. To stay and fight was impossible. So they embarked on a desperate, 1,300-mile flight toward a place of safety across the border in Canada, where they knew that the Lakota chief Sitting Bull had a camp along the White Mud River in King George's Land, in the Northwest Territories. They were pursued every step of the way by two thousand American soldiers commanded by General Howard. By a brilliant use of guerrilla tactics, the Nez Perce managed to survive four major battles and fourteen skirmishes. But when they were within thirty miles of the Canadian border, a fresh army, commanded by Colonel Nelson A. Miles, caught them unawares at Bear Paws.

Hemene Moxmox (Yellow Wolf), a warrior of Chief Joseph's band, later recalled the fierce, close-range battle that ensued.

> Bullets from everywhere! A big gun throwing bursting shells. From rifle pits, warriors returned shot for shot. Wild and stormy, the cold wind was thick with snow. Air filled with smoke of powder. Flash of guns through it all.

Anon.
Yellow Wolf
Date unknown

Yellow Wolf (Hemene Moxmox) was Chief Joseph's nephew; he lived long enough for Lucullus Virgil McWhorter, rancher and friend of the Nez Perce, to record his life story, giving the Nez Perce side of the war. Yellow Wolf was among those who did not surrender their guns along with Joseph but followed Chief White Bird to join Sitting Bull in Canada before returning to their homeland and surrendering piecemeal in 1878.

As the hidden sun traveled upward, the war did not weaken.

I felt the coming end. All for which we had suffered lost!

Thoughts came of the Wallowa where I grew up. Of my own country when only Indians were there. Of tipis along the bending river. Of the blue, clear lake, wide meadows with horse and cattle herds. From the mountain forests, voices seemed calling. I felt as dreaming. Not my living self.

By October 5, 1877, Chief Joseph had no choice but to surrender. Looking Glass was dead. Toohoolhoolzote was dead. Joseph's brother Ollokut was dead. The people were starving. The children were freezing to death. Chief Joseph told Colonel Miles, "I am tired; my heart is sick and sad. From where the sun now stands, I will fight no more forever."

Although some of Chief White Bird's band did escape to Sitting Bull in Canada, the Nez Perce War was over. Colonel Miles, who greatly admired Chief Joseph, promised him that the 418 people who surrendered (87 men, 184 women, and 147 children) would be allowed to return to the Nez Perce reservation at Lapwai. He was overruled, however, and Chief Joseph and his people were exiled first to the Indian Territory of Oklahoma and then to the Colville reservation in Washington State, where Chief Joseph died in 1904.

In 1895 forced division of the Nez Perce reservation into individual allotments of land opened it to white settlement, resulting in the loss of much of the land salvaged in the 1863 treaty. A tribal land base of over thirteen million acres in 1800 had been reduced to less than eighty thousand acres by 1975. In recent years, though, a tribal policy of reacquiring land has seen this figure rise.

By the 1930s the influence of Presbyterian Christianity on Nez Perce culture was receding in the face of a strong revival of traditional Nez Perce culture, including the re-introduction of the winter spirit dances, which had been banned by the reservation authorities for over fifty years. This process of reclaiming Nez Perce traditions and values continues today.

In 2004 the Nez Perce numbered 3,326. A general council of all adult members elects a tribal executive committee to administer health, education, housing, and economic programs, and oversee natural resources such as water and fish stocks.

For at least a generation after the defeat at Bear Paws, the reservation Nez Perces disowned the memory of Chief Joseph and his "hostiles." Gradually, his achievements were reassessed, and today he is revered as the hero of the struggle for Nez Perce independence.

White Americans admired Chief Joseph for his supposed military skills, hailing him as the Indian Napoleon. But in truth Chief Joseph was no military genius; he was a man of peace, not of war. The most vivid description of Chief Joseph in battle shows not a general directing his troops, or a warrior defying his enemy, but a weaponless non-combatant cradling a baby. The warrior Two Moons recalled him at the terrible Battle of Big Hole, where so many of the Nez Perce women and children were slaughtered.

> I rose up and ran up the creek for better shooting, when I met Chief Joseph. He spoke to me, "Remember I have no gun for defending myself." He was holding a little baby in his arms, so I said to him, "Skip for your life. Without the gun you can do nothing. Save the child!"

6 NOTHING LIVES LONG

Young men, help me, do help me!
I love my country so;
That is why I am fighting.

Sitting Bull (Tatanka Iyotanka), Hunkpapa Lakota

In the nineteenth century the Lakota lived in the buffalo country of the tall-grass prairies. They had been pushed north and west from the woodlands of Minnesota by Iroquoian and Algonquian tribes, who had traded furs for firearms with the French and the English. The Yankton Lakota crossed the Minnesota River onto the prairie around 1670, and the Teton and the Santee followed.

At this stage, the Lakota had neither horses nor guns. The change from a forest lifestyle—surviving on game from the woods and wild rice gathered from the marshes—to hunting buffalo on the plains was not easy. A new territory required new skills. The Lakota men had to learn to disguise themselves in wolf skins and sneak up on a buffalo herd, hoping to panic the animals and drive them over a cliff.

In Minnesota, the Lakota had lived in a state of constant rivalry and warfare with neighboring nations such as the Cree and the Ojibwe (Anishinaabe), and they brought this same aggressive attitude with them to the Great Plains, where they soon clashed with established nations like the Arikara, Mandan, and Pawnee. The Arikara, in particular, were a formidable barrier to the westward expansion of the Lakota. In 1760 the Arikara population numbered about twenty thousand, roughly twice that of the Lakota. And the Arikara lived in permanent villages, where they

David F. Barry
Sitting Bull 1885

Sitting Bull (c.1831–90) was both a war leader and a holy man of the Lakota. He is remembered as one of the greatest of all Indian chiefs. In 1877 he said, "I will remain what I am until I die, a hunter, and when there are no buffalo or other game I will send my children to hunt and live on prairie mice, for where an Indian is shut up in one place his body becomes weak."

91

*The Kiowa and the
Lakota were among the
peoples who kept simple
historical records in the
form of pictorial
calendars or "winter
counts." This image
recalls the "Smallpox
winter" of 1839–40, in
which many Kiowas,
Apaches, and
Comanches died. This
was part of the wider
smallpox epidemic that
began on the upper
Missouri in 1837 and
swept through the
Plains, killing around
a third of the Native
population. Some
nations, such as the
Mandan, were almost
wiped out.*

grew crops of corn, squash, and beans to supplement the buffalo caught on the communal spring and autumn hunts.

But it was the settled nature of their life that proved the downfall of nations such as the Arikara and the Mandan. Living close together and having frequent contact with whites, made them vulnerable to the white man's diseases, to which they had no resistance. Smallpox, scarlet fever, measles, and typhoid all took their toll. In the 1770s the Arikara suffered three major epidemics, which wiped out four-fifths of the population; eventually, the Arikara joined forces with the similarly depleted Mandan and Hidatsa as the Three Affiliated Tribes.

The Lakota, who traveled in small nomadic bands, suffered no such losses. Instead, during the years in which the Mandan were virtually wiped out by smallpox, the Lakota enjoyed a population explosion. From an estimated 8,500 in 1805, the Lakota population rose to 25,000 by 1850.

The key to this new prosperity was the horse. By 1800 the horse was a crucial part of Lakota life, and it had transformed both hunting and warfare. Horses had been introduced to the American southwest by the Spanish but did not become part of Native American culture until after the Pueblo Revolt of 1680, during which the Pueblo Indians drove the Spanish from New Mexico and acquired their huge horse herds. Horses were not of much use in the settled pueblos, and they were traded away to nomadic peoples such as the Apache, Ute, and Navajo. From there they spread across the country. The Lakota got their first horses from the Cheyenne, one of the few tribes with whom they were on consistently friendly terms.

By 1820 the Lakota dominated the Plains. They drove their enemies the Crow from their Powder River hunting lands in Wyoming, claimed the South Dakota Badlands, and found a focus for their strong spiritual yearnings in the sacred mountains of the Black Hills, which they called Paha

Sapa, also in South Dakota. Paha Sapa was the site of the creation of mankind. It was there that, in the Creation time, the birds (representing the two-legged creatures, including humans) raced against the four-legged animals in order to establish supremacy. The birds won, giving humans the right to hunt animals such as the buffalo for food.

The idea of deciding such a matter by means of a contest of skill and strength is typical of the Lakota. This people valued four virtues above all: bravery, fortitude, generosity, and wisdom. Lakota boys were brought up in an atmosphere of intense competition and rivalry. They learned early both to endure and to inflict pain. A young man of the Lakota was not thought fit to marry until he had killed an enemy; bravery and skill in warfare were the measure of a man, and the primary source of status in Lakota society. For gentler souls there was an alternative: They could become *winkte,* wearing women's clothing and sharing the women's chores, but with the status of a medicine man.

This warrior culture made the Lakota formidable enemies.

Edward Sheriff Curtis
Piegan travois 1911

The Plains nations used a wooden sledge known as a travois to transport camp equipment and also the sick and elderly. Before the acquisition of horses, smaller travois were hauled by dogs.

When the Lakota and whites eventually clashed, it was clear that the Lakota idea of warfare was very different from that of the whites. For the Lakota, a war party offered individual warriors the chance to display their bravery, and thus acquire honors and status. The greater the risk, the braver the act.

In a battle, each warrior wanted more than anything to "count coup" on an enemy. This meant to touch the enemy's body, often with a special coup stick. Although it was acceptable to count coup on a corpse, it was braver to touch a living man than a dead one. Many of the battle rituals in which the Lakota warriors displayed their courage—for instance, counting coup or riding in circles ever closer to the enemy and showing off their horsemanship—made them easy targets for U.S. soldiers with rapid-fire breech-loading rifles or multibarreled Gatling guns.

Until the 1850s, when the Santee lost their land and were settled on a reservation, the Lakota had not felt especially threatened by white encroachment. Although the Lakota had experienced conflict with the whites, they were much more interested in fighting against other tribes, because the two aims of warfare were to acquire battle honors and to steal the enemy's horses. Intertribal warfare was an essential component of both ceremonial and economic life. Because the Lakota did not at first regard the whites as a threat, they did not formally classify them as enemies and therefore could not acquire battle honors by fighting them.

The Lakota established trade links with French whites as early as the mid–seventeenth century, but their traditional way of life remained unaffected. The Lakota, in fact, actively sought to interact with the white man; in 1695 a Lakota chief traveled to Montreal to ask the governor of New France to send more traders to the Lakota villages.

Perhaps inevitably it was the easternmost Lakota, the

Joel Emmons Whitney
A group of Dakota Indians in front of a settler's brick building, on the day the Sioux revolt commenced 1862

These Dakota (Santee) Indians are wearing mostly western dress, indicating the extent to which the Santee had adopted the white man's ways. The photo was presumably taken on August 17, 1862, the day a group of four young Santee men, eager to prove their bravery, massacred settler Robinson Jones, his wife, his adopted daughter, and two other men in Acton township, Meeker County. The "Acton Massacre" sparked the Sioux Uprising. When Little Crow heard of it, he understood at once that "the whites would take a dreadful vengeance because women had been killed."

Santee, who first faced the harsh reality of the inevitable conflict between the aims and values of the Indians and the whites. In 1830 the Santee signed the first of a series of treaties that over the course of thirty years deprived them of most of their land, reducing them from independence to destitution. By 1853 they were settled in a reservation along the Minnesota River. Although some Santees converted to Christianity and tried to take up agriculture, poverty and hunger made many bitter and resentful.

These resentments boiled over in 1862 in hostilities that became known as the Sioux Uprising. The Santee had already lost nine-tenths of their land, and the game on which they relied for food was almost gone. In July 1862 the Santee were starving. The agency warehouse on their reservation was full of food, but the government annuities that would pay for it had been delayed, and the agent refused to release the food before he was paid. A Santee chief, Little Crow (Taoyateduta), said, "We have waited a long time. The money is ours, but we cannot get it. We have no food, but here are these stores, filled with food."

The agent asked some white traders what he should do.

One of them, Andrew Myrick, said, "So far as I am concerned, if they are hungry let them eat grass or their own dung."

When four frustrated young Santees killed five settlers, Little Crow was angry. "Kill one—two—ten, and ten times ten will come to kill you," he said. He knew that the die was cast. To show he was not a coward, he led an attack on the agency. Ten whites were killed. Among them was Andrew Myrick, whose body was left with his mouth stuffed with grass.

For a month Little Crow and his warriors held their own against the whites, but as fresh troops poured into Minnesota to deal with the uprising, Little Crow's earlier words were proved right. "White men with guns . . . will come faster than you can count." The Santee were brutally crushed, and thirty-eight picked out as ringleaders were hanged at Mankato, Minnesota, on December 26, 1862. These included two who were executed "by mistake."

One of these was a man known as Chaska. His case was unusual because, at the perfunctory trials the Santees were allowed, a white woman who had been his captive, Sarah Wakefield, exposed herself to ridicule and scandal by testifying in his defense. Far from being a bloodthirsty savage, Chaska had saved her life, and her children's lives, and treated her with kindness: "They are poor, he and his family—They have had to beg victuals for me and my children and gone without himself. He is a very generous man. I have seen him give away his own shirt to Indians."

Sarah Wakefield's testimony may have sealed Chaska's fate. The climate of public opinion allowed Santees to be portrayed only as "savage murderers," "ravishers," and "hideous wretches." Sarah's loyalty to Chaska, her obvious admiration for him, and the suspicion that she had fallen in love with her captor appalled the court. It seems clear that when Chaska was hanged, it was no mistake but a way of

after Charles Bird King
Little Crow 1835–36

Thomas J. Galbraith was awarded the post of Indian agent for services to the Republicans in the election of 1860. Little Crow attributed the Sioux Uprising, which he reluctantly led, to Galbraith's incompetence. Galbraith insisted on sticking to the letter of the rules and refused to distribute food to the hungry Santee before the annuity payments arrived. Little Crow said to him, "We ask that you, the agent, make some arrangement by which we can get food from the stores, or else we may take our own way to keep ourselves from starving. When men are hungry they help themselves." After the uprising, Little Crow escaped to Canada, but he was killed by bounty hunters in 1863 while picking raspberries with his son.

96

bringing the whole embarrassing affair to a decisive end. The next day the marshal of the prison went to release Chaska and was told, "You hung him yesterday."

The other prisoner hanged "in error" was a sixteen-year-old white boy who had been brought up among the Santee, another threat to the simple division between the savage and the civilized.

After this, one group of the Santee was pushed from one unsuitable reservation to another, while the rest fled to the Plains. There some of them joined forces with their Teton and Yankton cousins, who were by this time already in conflict with the whites.

One persistent problem was the difference in power structures and social relations between the Lakota and the whites. On the government side, commissioners understandably wished to have a single chief with whom they could deal. But this ran counter to Lakota tradition. Authority resided in the councils and chiefs of each lodge group or band, each of which consisted of ten to twenty families, or fifty to one hundred people. In 1851, negotiating the Treaty of Horse Creek, South Dakota, the commissioners brushed aside Lakota objections and appointed a Sichangu chief, Frightening Bear, as head chief. When in 1854 a white settler complained at Fort Laramie, Wyoming, that a Lakota from Frightening Bear's camp had killed his cow, soldiers were sent to demand that the head chief surrender the guilty man. The man who had killed the cow, however, was not a Sichangu but a Mnikowoju, and Frightening Bear had no authority over him. Failing to understand this, Lieutenant John L. Grattan ordered his men to open fire with a howitzer, killing Frightening Bear. Grattan intended to frighten the Lakota into submission. It did not work. Within minutes Grattan and all twenty-nine men under his command were dead, and the Sichangu were on the warpath.

Joel Emmons Whitney
Little Six 1865

Little Six (Shakopee), a prominent Mdewakanton Dakota, was a delegate to Washington in 1858. The young men who perpetrated the Acton Massacre were members of a band that had seceded from Little Six's village. Little Six was among those hanged at Mankato, Minnesota, as leaders of the 1862 Sioux Uprising. His name survives in the Little Six Bingo Palace on today's Shakopee Mdewakanton Reservation in Minnesota. The gambling hall opened in 1982 and grossed over 9 million dollars in its first year.

Over the course of the next two years, the death of that one cow led to many deaths among the whites and the Lakotas, including the massacre at Blue Water Creek, Wyoming, of a Sichangu village led by Little Thunder, at which eighty-six Lakotas were killed and seventy women and children taken prisoner. But the massacre that finally lit the fuse for all-out war on the Plains was not of Lakotas but Cheyennes. It happened at Sand Creek, Colorado, early in the morning on November 29, 1864. Colonel John Chivington attacked the camp of the friendly Cheyenne chief Black Kettle with a force of seven hundred volunteer militiamen, many of whom were violent Indian haters. Chivington, a former Methodist preacher, left them in no doubt where he stood: "Damn any man who sympathizes with Indians!" he declared. "I have come to kill Indians, and believe it is right and honorable to use any means under God's heaven to kill Indians."

George Bent, the son of white trader William Bent and his Cheyenne wife, Owl Woman, was there.

> At dawn on the morning of November 29 I was still in bed when I heard shouts and the noise of people running about the camp. I jumped up and ran out of my lodge. From down the creek a large body of troops was advancing at a rapid trot, some to the east of the camp, and others on the opposing side of the creek, to the west. More soldiers could be seen making for the Indian pony herds to the south of the camps; in the camps themselves all was confusion and noise—men, women, and children rushing out of the lodges partly dressed; women and children screaming at sight of the troops; men running back into the lodges for their arms, other men, already armed, or with lassos and bridles in their hands, running for the herds to attempt to get some of the ponies before the troops could reach the animals and drive them off. I looked toward the chief's lodge and saw that Black Kettle had a large American flag tied to the end of a long lodgepole and was standing in front of his lodge, holding the pole, with the flag fluttering in the

© Colorado Historical Society

Anon.
George Bent with his wife, Magpie
Date unknown

George Bent's father, Colonel William Bent, owned and operated Bent's Fort on the Upper Arkansas River in southeastern Colorado. His mother, Owl Woman, was the daughter of White Thunder; as keeper of the sacred Medicine Arrows, White Thunder was considered more important than any of the chiefs of the Southern Cheyenne. His wife, Magpie, was the niece of Black Kettle, the chief whose camp was attacked at Sand Creek, and both she and her husband were eyewitnesses to the massacre. The night after the attack was remembered by Bent as "the worst night I ever went through....The men and women who were not wounded worked all through the night, trying to keep the children and the wounded from freezing to death."

gray light of the winter dawn. I heard him call to the people not to be afraid, that the soldiers would not hurt them; then the troops opened fire from two sides of the camp.

A second chief in the camp, White Antelope, had been to Washington with Black Kettle in 1863 and, like him, believed in friendship and peace with the whites. White Antelope did not fight, but simply stood outside his lodge with his arms folded across his chest, singing his death song.

> Nothing lives long,
> Only the earth and the mountains.

Chivington especially encouraged his men to kill Indian children, and many women and children were among the 137 killed. Their bodies were then grotesquely mutilated. The frontier whites regarded this massacre as a great victory. At a Denver, Colorado, theater the band played patriotic songs while a group of Chivington's militiamen displayed the scalps of a hundred Cheyennes, mostly women and children, to a wildly cheering crowd.

The reaction on the Plains was very different. The atrocity at Sand Creek caused the Lakota, Cheyenne, and Arapaho to band together on the warpath. That winter a messenger went around all the Lakota winter camps, uniting them to fight the whites. Among those who argued for war was the Oglala chief Red Cloud.

The whites were formally declared enemies, meaning that a Lakota warrior who counted coup on a white man now earned the same prestige as one who performed the same symbolic feat of bravery in an intertribal war. This subtle change of status profoundly changed the Lakota attitude to the whites. From now on, Lakota warriors were not simply protecting themselves against white attack, or retaliating for provocation; they were engaged in acts of war that would earn them honor and status among their people.

In 1866 Red Cloud led his people in a brilliant guerrilla campaign against the forts on the Bozeman Trail, a shortcut from the Oregon Trail to the gold fields of Montana that passed through the Teton hunting grounds on the Powder River. "For my part," Red Cloud said, "I prefer to die fighting rather than by starvation."

One brash young cavalry captain, William J. Fetterman, was particularly impatient with the army's lack of progress in subduing the Lakota, and was heard to boast that he

could ride through the entire Sioux Nation with eighty men. In December 1866 a force of eighty men under Fetterman was completely annihilated. This incident was always referred to by whites as the Fetterman Massacre, although all his troops were armed and actively engaged in hostilities, unlike the Cheyenne women and children at Sand Creek. There was one gruesome similarity between the two "massacres": In revenge for Sand Creek, the Lakota and Cheyenne warriors scalped and mutilated the bodies of Fetterman's troops.

Red Cloud himself was probably not directly involved in the Fetterman fight, in which the war leaders were the Mnikowoju chief High Back Bone and a young Oglala called Crazy Horse. Crazy Horse was an unusual young man, solitary and self-possessed, who was regarded by his own people as "strange." He did not dance the Sun Dance, he did not take scalps, he did not count coup—instead, he killed his enemies, with ruthless, intense efficiency.

The Fetterman fight was the climax of Red Cloud's War.

Alexander Gardner
Lakota chiefs at Fort Laramie 1868

These chiefs were photographed during a break in peace negotiations that Red Cloud refused to attend. From left to right: Spotted Tail, Roman Nose, Old Man Afraid of His Horses, Long Horn, Whistling Elk, Pipe, and Slow Bull.

Trager and Kuhn
Red Cloud
Date unknown

Red Cloud normally posed for the camera in traditional dress, with a single eagle feather in his hair. Here he wears western clothes—a suit, starched shirt, stiff collar, and bow tie. He understood that, when negotiating, wearing white men's clothes put him on a more equal footing with those who might otherwise dismiss him as a savage.

Perhaps surprisingly, it was not followed by ferocious reprisals. Instead, it led to the formation in July 1867 of the Indian Peace Commission, a federal body charged with removing the causes of hostilities on the Plains, and thereby ensuring the smooth progress of the planned transcontinental railroad.

The Peace Commission announced new treaty talks at Fort Laramie—but Red Cloud refused to attend. He sent the commissioners a message, telling them bluntly that he would not make peace until the forts along the Powder River were abandoned. "I mean to keep this land," he said.

The Peace Commissioners returned to Fort Laramie in the spring of 1868, ready to agree to Red Cloud's terms. But still he would not sit down with them. He sent them another message: "We are on the mountains looking down on the soldiers and the forts," it read. "When we see the soldiers moving away and the forts abandoned, then I will come down and talk." That summer the troops were withdrawn from Forts F. C. Smith, Phil Kearny, and Reno. No sooner were they gone than Red Cloud's warriors razed the forts to the ground.

For the first and only time, Native Americans had won not just a battle but a war with the whites. When Red Cloud rode into Fort Laramie that November to sign a peace treaty, which apparently gave him everything for which he had been fighting, he had good cause to feel pleased with himself.

In 1870 Red Cloud was invited to Washington to meet President Ulysses S. Grant, the Great Father. The invitation came from the Commissioner of Indian Affairs. For the first time, this crucial post was being filled by an Indian, Ely S. Parker, or Donehogawa, a Seneca, who had made his name at Grant's side in the Civil War.

Unfortunately, when Parker went through the terms of the 1868 treaty with Red Cloud, it became clear that the Great Sioux Reservation in South Dakota would not after all include the prime hunting grounds of the Powder River. Red Cloud had been deceived. He refused to take a copy of the treaty, saying, "It is all lies."

Parker managed to smooth things over by broadening the interpretation of the treaty, so that Red Cloud and his people would be allowed to live and hunt along the Powder River. On his way home Red Cloud visited New York and gave a celebrated speech at the Cooper Union. "All I want is right and justice," he said.

When Red Cloud returned to his people, he was as

enthusiastic for peace as he had been for war. Perhaps he trusted the good intentions of Ely Parker and President Grant; perhaps the displays of U.S. might he had seen in Washington had convinced him that armed resistance was futile; perhaps, as some Lakota muttered, the "shadow catchers" who had taken his photograph in the capital had somehow stolen his soul. Crazy Horse, at least, thought something of the kind; he alone of all the great chiefs of his time would never allow himself to be photographed.

Nor would Crazy Horse be persuaded to make peace. Now that Red Cloud had given up the fight, Crazy Horse took his band to join the Hunkpapa chief Sitting Bull. Sitting Bull was a war chief and also a spiritual leader, and he and Crazy Horse made a potent partnership. Soon they were to inflict the greatest blow to American pride in the entire history of the Indian wars.

The latest cause for conflict was the whites' demand that the Lakota give up their sacred Black Hills. In the summer of 1874 Lieutenant Colonel George A. Custer led a military expedition to explore the Black Hills. Their report of significant gold deposits in the hills prompted a gold rush on the Great Sioux Reservation. But the Lakota stubbornly refused to sell. The Black Hills were, they explained, "the heart of everything that is."

In June 1876 an encampment of some seven thousand Lakota, representing all seven Lakota tribes in six tribal circles (the Blackfeet and Two Kettles were combined), converged along the Little Big Horn River in Wyoming. Among the chiefs were Sitting Bull and Crazy Horse. At a Sun Dance ceremony Sitting Bull ritually cut one hundred pieces of flesh from his arms and danced the sun-gazing dance. His act of sacrifice was rewarded with a vision: "Many soldiers falling into the camp."

The many soldiers who were to fall into the camp were led by George Custer. He was determined to crush the

Edward Sheriff Curtis
On the Little Big Horn 1909

This Apsaroke (Crow) camp is situated on the Little Big Horn River, Montana, a short distance below the site of the Custer fight.

Lakota, because he was sure that the fame he would win by doing so would secure him the presidency. And so on June 25, 1876, Custer engaged Sitting Bull in the Battle of the Little Big Horn. This battle became known as Custer's Last Stand, because the warriors under Sitting Bull and Crazy Horse killed Custer and every man under his command. The Lakota chief Runs-the-Enemy later recalled, "When the last soldier was killed the smoke rolled up like a mountain above our heads, and the soldiers were piled one on top of another, dead, and here and there an Indian among the soldiers."

But even a crushing victory like this could not turn back the tide of history. By May the following year Sitting Bull and his band were exiled in Canada, where they were to remain peacefully for four years. Crazy Horse and his band were being relentlessly pursued by soldiers under the command of Colonel Nelson A. Miles. And in the meantime Red Cloud and other treaty chiefs had signed an agreement ceding the Black Hills, and had been disarmed. General George Crook, who was in overall command of the U.S. forces, declared that Red Cloud was no longer the chief of the Oglala; he would deal only with the more malleable Sichangu chief Spotted Tail.

It may have been this last humiliation that persuaded Red Cloud to cooperate with the U.S. soldiers in bringing in Crazy Horse. Red Cloud was jealous of the younger man's popularity, and there had been bad blood between them since Crazy Horse had been thwarted in his love for Red Cloud's niece, Black Buffalo Woman. Whatever the truth of the matter, Red Cloud brought Crazy Horse in to surrender on May 6, 1877. The Great Sioux War was over.

The charismatic Crazy Horse was to live only another four months. When soldiers tried to put him in a cell, he resisted and received a bayonet thrust through the back. It was an end that would find an echo on December 16, 1890, when Sitting Bull was killed by Indian police sent to arrest him.

Sitting Bull had surrendered in 1881, but he was still feared by the whites. He was killed because of worries over a new religious movement, the Ghost Dance. This revival of traditional religious beliefs spread like wildfire from the Great Basin across the Plains in 1889. It originated among the northern Paiute or Numu, and its prophet was a man named Wovoka, known to the whites as Jack Wilson. Wovoka's father had been a follower of the earlier, similar Ghost Dance movement of 1870, which also originated among the Paiute.

On January 1, 1889, Wovoka had what today we would call a near-death experience, possibly triggered by scarlet fever. While cutting wood in the mountains, Wovoka heard

James Mooney
Wovoka with Charley Sheep 1892

Wovoka, the prophet of the 1890 Ghost Dance, is shown here with his sombrero and sacred eagle feather. Standing behind him is his uncle, Charley Sheep. Despite the tragic failure of the Ghost Dance movement, Wovoka remained true to his own vision, believing himself destined to be "President of the West." When a Sac-Fox Indian, Charles Curtis, became Herbert Hoover's vice president in 1929, Wovoka sent him a telegram of congratulations, perhaps anticipating that his revelation might soon be fulfilled.

a great noise from above and fell into a coma or trance, during which he was granted the first of three visions of heaven. Captain James Josephus, a Paiute member of the Indian police, who was a firm believer in the man he called "the new Christ," reported, "He laid down his ax and started to go in the direction of the noise, when he fell down dead; and that God came and took him to heaven and showed him everything there."

The sun was addressed by the Paiutes as Our Father and was equated with the Creator, Wolf. Wovoka's vision took place during a solar eclipse. Wovoka was believed to have died, to have talked with God, to have saved the world by preventing the moon from devouring the sun, and then to have come back to life again. God made Wovoka the messiah of a new religion, in which the world would be renewed by dancing the Ghost Dance (based on the traditional Paiute Round Dance) in five-day festivals. The Ghost Dancers believed that the re-created world would come in a whirlwind from the west, with the messiah and their resurrected relatives upon it, and slowly cover the old, exhausted earth, providing a new "heaven on earth" for the faithful. The wicked (whom many identified as the whites) would be pushed into the sea. Soon the belief spread that the new world would be established in the spring of 1891 when the grass was an inch high.

When the War Department heard of this new religion, they sent an Indian scout, Arthur I. Chapman, to investigate. Wovoka met him on December 4, 1890, and told him matter-of-factly that God "gave him the power to destroy this world and all the people in it and have it made over again."

While Wovoka's teaching borrowed elements from Christianity and other white faiths, it was profoundly rooted in the traditional religion of the Paiute. In essence, his message of the renewal of the Indian world repeated that of the prophet of the 1870 Ghost Dance, Wodziwob.

Like Wodziwob, Wovoka was a man of great spiritual power. He could, it was said, light his pipe from the sun and form icicles in his hand. He was also said to be invulnerable to bullets, and he staged demonstrations in which others shot at him and he then took off his shirt to show bullet holes but no injuries. Wovoka's displays of invulnerability were to have a tragic consequence. The Lakota, transferring the prophet's power to themselves, took to wearing special Ghost shirts, which they believed could not be penetrated by bullets.

A young Lakota holy man, Black Elk, was one of those

captivated by the stories of a man who could show "the whole world and all that was wonderful" inside his upturned hat. Black Elk joined the Ghost Dance movement, and he had a vision of "a beautiful land where many, many people were camping in a great circle, I could see that they were happy and had plenty. Everywhere there were drying racks full of meat. The air was clear and beautiful with a living light that was everywhere." In his vision Black Elk saw how to make the special shirts that would keep his people safe.

Wovoka's new religion had a strong appeal. Just as Tenskwatawa's prophecies sustained the campaigns of his brother Tecumseh, and Smohalla's Dreamer religion united the Nez Perce in their struggles with the government in the 1870s, so the Ghost Dance gave the Lakota new hope that they might even yet prevail.

The element of Wovoka's teaching that appealed above all was his insistence that in the new world the buffalo would come back. The government policy of exterminating the buffalo had driven the Lakota to the edge of starvation and threatened to destroy the basis of their religion and their culture. Between 1877 and 1884, in a deliberate attempt to starve the people of the Plains into submission, white buffalo hunters such as Buffalo Bill Cody were promised by the government 160 acres of land for every one hundred buffalo hides. More than twenty million buffalo were slaughtered and left to rot on the prairie, and by the time of the Ghost Dance there were only about a thousand animals left in the wild.

With the Ghost Dance, all the Lakota had to do was dance and wait, and their traditional world would be remade. Wovoka's message was clear: "There must be peace all over the world." But to the whites, the Ghost Dance—even though women were taking part in it— seemed like a war dance. So Sitting Bull was killed (although he was not, in fact, a believer in Wovoka's vision), and the scene was set for the last tragic act of the Indian wars.

On December 29, 1890, a group of approximately 300 Mnikowoju Lakota, whose chief was Big Foot, or Si Tanka, came in to surrender to the U.S. military at Wounded Knee. Many of them were wearing the special Ghost shirts that Black Elk had seen in his vision. They believed that these shirts, painted with the sun, moon, stars, the eagle, the crow, and the buffalo, would keep them—men, women, and children—safe from the guns of the whites.

All was going smoothly until, in a minor scuffle, one warrior's gun fired into the air. Immediately, the soldiers of the 7th Cavalry opened fire on the mostly unarmed Indians. More than 146 were killed, and many more were injured. At the Pine Ridge Reservation in South Dakota, one of five smaller reservations created when the Great Sioux Reservation was broken up in 1889 to allow the Northern Pacific Railway to push through the old reservation lands, a makeshift field hospital was set up to tend the wounded. Among the doctors was a Santee named Ohiyesa, who as Charles A. Eastman was one of the first Lakota to effectively

enter the white man's world, initially as a doctor and then as an author. One injured woman was asked whether they might remove her Ghost shirt. "Yes, take it off," she replied. "They told me a bullet would not go through. Now I don't want it any more."

Even so, neither the Paiute prophet Wovoka nor the Lakota holy man Black Elk ever lost faith in the great vision of redemption each had been granted, a vision of a world in which the broken hoop of the Indian nations would be remade. It was a world promised in so many of the simple, yearning Ghost Dance songs.

> I love my children—*Ye'ye'!*
> I love my children—*Ye'ye'!*
> You shall grow to be a nation—*Ye'ye'!*
> You shall grow to be a nation—*Ye'ye'!*
> Says the father, says the father.
> *Haye'ye' E'yayo'yo! Haye'ye' E'yayo'yo!*

7 ONE WITH THIS WORLD

My friend, I am old, but I shall never die. I shall always live in my children, and children's children.

New Corn (Potawatomi), 1795

On February 17, 1909, the great Apache freedom fighter Goyathlay—known to the whites as Geronimo—died of pneumonia at Fort Sill, Oklahoma. He had been a prisoner of war since surrendering to General Nelson A. Miles in 1886. It seemed that, from the east coast to the west and across the Great Plains in between, not just Indian resistance but the very spirit of the Indians had been crushed.

In those wasted years, Geronimo did one notable thing. He wrote—or rather dictated—his autobiography. He was by no means the first Native American to do so, but his action is still significant, for it was by putting their experience and their knowledge into written words that Native Americans began to reclaim and redefine their culture and values.

In 1864, nine years before he became the first Indian commissioner of Indian Affairs, the Seneca Ely S. Parker (Donehogawa) wrote a long letter to General Ulysses S. Grant containing his thoughts on how best to ensure peace and harmony in Indian-white relations. He concluded,

> The American government can never adopt the policy of a total extermination of the Indian race within her limits, numbering, perhaps, less than four hundred thousand, without a cost of untold treasure and lives of her people, besides exposing herself to the abhorrence and censure of the entire civilized world.

Just eight months later Colonel John Chivington led his troops in the Sand Creek Massacre of the peaceful village

Ilka Hartmann
Intertribal Friendship House
1972

This Indian center in Oakland, California, was owned by the Quakers but governed by Indians; in 2003 it was sold to the Indians. It is a place for Indians to gather, and to get referrals to government agencies. Standing in front are Sarah Brown, a Pomo, with her niece Tina and nephew Anthony Fourkiller. The American Quakers have been staunch supporters of Indian rights since the days of William Penn.

113

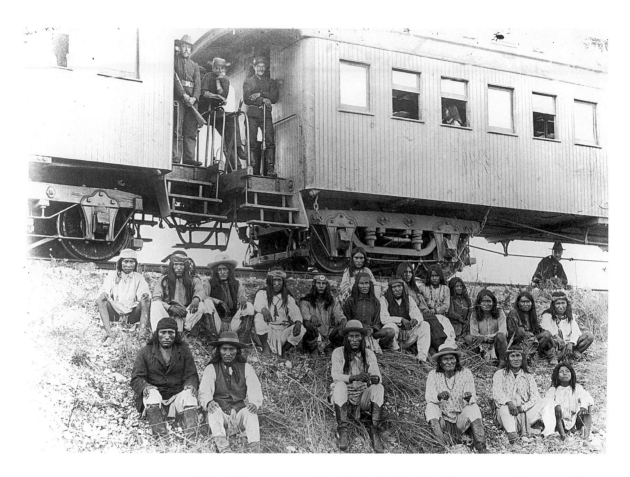

A. J. Macdonald
Apache prisoners in transit 1886

This photograph shows prisoners from Geronimo's band in transit to Fort Sam Houston, Texas, and Fort Marion, Florida. From left to right in the front row are Geronimo's cousins Fun and Perico; Cochise's son, Naiche; Geronimo; Geronimo's son, Chappo, and an orphan boy, Garditha.

of the Cheyenne chief Black Kettle. He certainly would not have agreed with Parker. He shared the views of Governor John R. Baylor—the governor of the Arizona Territory, then part of the Confederacy—who wrote to the commander of the Arizona guards in 1862:

> I learn from Lieutenant J. J. Jackson that Indians have been in your post for the purpose of making a treaty. The Congress of the Confederate States has passed a law declaring extermination to all hostile Indians. You will therefore use all means to persuade the Apaches or any tribe to come in for the purpose of making peace, and when you get them together kill all the grown Indians and take the children prisoners and sell them to defray the expense of killing the Indians.

At the time Geronimo told his story, it was assumed by whites that the Indians were on the point of cultural extinction. The remnants of the First Nations were confined to reservations and reduced to poverty. Soon they would "vanish" by assimilation into the mainstream white culture.

Over the course of the twentieth century, this assumption was proved mistaken, as Indians across North America proudly reclaimed their cultural heritage. Holy men and women, community leaders, political activists, writers, artists, and poets have been remaking the sacred hoop that was broken at Wounded Knee.

One force among many in this process was the autobiography of Black Elk, as told to the poet John G. Neihardt. Black Elk was three years old when his second cousin Crazy Horse lured Captain Fetterman and his men to their deaths in the Fetterman Massacre. He was a witness to the massacre at Wounded Knee, and narrowly escaped death there himself. Speaking to Neihardt in 1931 about the immediate aftermath of Wounded Knee, Black Elk recalled sitting in a tipi with another Lakota, named Red Crow, and eating *papa* (dried buffalo meat).

> As we were feasting there about three feet apart we heard some shots and just then the bullet went right between us and threw dust over our plates. We kept on eating anyway and had our fill and we got on our horses and went the way the people had fled. Probably if I had been killed there I would have had *papa* in my mouth.

There is a yearning quality to this memory, a reaching back to a lost world. But Black Elk did not die that day; he lived another sixty years.

Although he had been a shaman, or medicine man, and remained guided by the great vision of his childhood, Black Elk did not live solely in the traditional past of his people, as Neihardt's wonderful book based on his memories might suggest. In December 1904 Black Elk was received into the Roman Catholic church by the Holy Rosary

Rev. Joseph Zimmerman S.J. **Mass at St. Elizabeth's Church, Oglala** 1936

Nicholas Black Elk is shown sitting front right, wearing glasses. Black Elk's Catholic beliefs were heartfelt, and they existed alongside his more deeply rooted Lakota spirituality.

Mission at Pine Ridge and baptized Nicholas Black Elk. From then on he was known as Nick Black Elk, and he devoted much of his time to instructing fellow Lakotas in Catholic beliefs.

Even before Wounded Knee, Black Elk had been intrigued by Christianity. His letters home from Europe, where he traveled with Buffalo Bill's Wild West show in 1888–89, speak of a wish to visit the Holy Land, to see for himself the place "where they killed Jesus." No wonder he was intrigued when he heard that Jesus had come again, but this time to the Indians in the form of the Ghost Dance prophet Wovoka.

After Wounded Knee, Black Elk, like many Lakotas, turned away from the white man's ways. He devoted himself to serving his people as a medicine man. This brought him into conflict with missionaries; on one occasion, a Jesuit priest is said to have interrupted Black Elk during a healing ceremony and destroyed the sacred objects he was using.

The reasons for Black Elk's conversion are not clear, but he was certainly sincere in his Catholic faith, and he was personally responsible for around four hundred conversions. He wrote in the *Catholic Herald* of July 1908:

Those of us here on earth who are suffering should help one another and have pity. We belong to one family and we have only one faith. Therefore, those who are suffering, my relatives, we should look toward them and pray for them, because our Savior came on this earth and helped all poor people.

Nick Black Elk was held up by the reservation authorities as an example to all of the way in which traditional Indians could turn their backs on superstition and embrace civilization. When John G. Neihardt visited him in 1930, hoping to talk to him about the Ghost Dance and Crazy Horse, it seemed unlikely he would get very far with the pious Catholic. But Black Elk simply looked at him and said, "As I sit here, I can feel in this man beside me a strong desire to know the things of the Other World. He has been sent to learn what I know, and I will teach him."

"What I know" turned out to have nothing to do with Black Elk's Catholic faith. Instead, it was the first true revelation of traditional Lakota religion. At the heart of the book is the story of Black Elk's power vision, which came to him when he was nine years old. "What I know was given to me for men," Black Elk said, "and it is true and it is beautiful."

Black Elk remained a Catholic, but from his first meeting with Neihardt until his death, he sought also to reveal to the world the richness and the truth of his Lakota heritage. Neihardt's book *Black Elk Speaks* has been called "a North American bible of all tribes." In his later *The Sacred Pipe: Black Elk's Account of the Seven Rites of the Oglala Sioux,* Black Elk also provided a Lakota equivalent of the seven sacraments of the Catholic church. Black Elk's attempt to reconcile the Lakota and Christian truths was deeply felt. He did not give up his traditional beliefs when he accepted Christianity; instead, he found a way to integrate the two belief systems.

A fellow Oglala, George Sword, also gave up being a *wicasa wakan*, or holy man, to embrace Christianity. Sword became a deacon of the Episcopal church, as committed to the Protestant path as Black Elk was to the Catholic. George Sword too made a huge contribution to the preservation and understanding of traditional Lakota religion. Collaborating with a white man, James R. Walker, a government doctor on the Pine Ridge Reservation, Sword persuaded the Lakota holy men to share their sacred knowledge, so that "future generations of the Oglalas should be informed as to all that their ancestors believed and practiced."

In choosing John G. Neihardt and James R. Walker to be the vehicles for their sacred knowledge, Black Elk and George Sword did not misplace their trust. For Native Americans brought up in a society without reading or writing, the only way to keep such knowledge safe for future generations, in the face of cultural disintegration, was to find a sympathetic outsider to write it down. Many holders of sacred knowledge followed this route, with varying degrees of success, depending on the sympathetic intelligence and scholarship of the chosen scribe.

Most white writers who undertook such work made great efforts to record faithfully not just the words but the true meaning and spirit of what they were told. But they were still writing from outside looking in. As Native Americans took advantage of new educational opportunities, they moved from being informants and collaborators to becoming the acknowledged authorities on their own cultures. Native anthropologists made incomparable contributions to both the recording and the understanding of nations such as the Seneca, Yankton Lakota, Nez Perce, and Pawnee. It is probable that no one else could ever have persuaded some of the last traditional priests to unfold their secrets in such intimate detail.

Prominent among the Native anthropologists was Francis La Flesche, an Omaha. His achievement demonstrates a creative blending of Indian and white values that reflects his upbringing. He was one of several high-achieving children of Joseph La Flesche (Inshtamaza: Iron Eye), one of the two principal chiefs of the Omaha before he converted to Presbyterianism in the late 1850s. Joseph remained a leading figure among the Omaha, especially among those who believed that the path forward was to adopt the white man's way. He was the first Plains Indian to construct his own two-story frame house, in 1857, and soon a farming settlement grew up around it that the traditionalist Omaha referred to scathingly as "The Village of the Make-Believe White Men." His children were sent to the reservation's Presbyterian mission school.

Joseph refused to have his daughters tattooed with the Omaha "mark of honor" to which they were entitled (a sun on the forehead representing the male day, and a four-pointed star on the upper chest symbolizing the female night and the four life-giving winds). When asked why, he said:

> I was always sure that my sons and daughters would live to see the time when they would have to mingle with the white people, and I determined that they should not have any mark put upon them that might be detrimental in their future surroundings.

His daughter Susan La Flesche Picotte (1865–1915) was the first Native American woman to become a physician, graduating from the Women's Medical College in Philadelphia in 1889, at the head of a class of thirty-three students. Tattoos that were a mark of superior social status to the Omaha would have seemed a mark of inferiority to her fellow students.

Joseph La Flesche was a modernizer, a man who foresaw that, with the disappearance of the buffalo, the old ways of

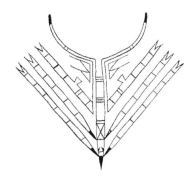

Osage tattoo recorded 1897

This design shows the "mark of honor" traditionally tattooed on the neck and chest of an Osage warrior; the Osage are related to the Omaha, and were once part of the same tribe. The meaning of the design is "The Sacred Pipe has descended." Among the Omaha, the mark of honor was granted not for deeds of war but for acts of peace and feats of hunting.

Anon.
Joseph La Flesche
Date unknown

Joseph La Flesche (1822-88) was raised by his mother, Watunna, among the Omaha, but his father was a French trader for the Hudson's Bay Company. Joseph knew his father well, often accompanying him on trading or hunting trips, and he spoke both French and English. Joseph's conversion to Christianity cost him his position as chief of the Omaha. However, he did not abandon all Omaha traditions; notably, he maintained three wives. His first wife, Mary, was the mother of Susette, the campaigner for Indian rights; his second wife, Tainne, was the mother of Francis, the anthropologist.

the Omaha would also disappear. The Indian looks into the future, he wrote, "and sees his only chance is to become as the white man." Yet his children were not so sure that the answer was to try to turn Indians into whites. Another of his daughters, Susette (also known as Yosette), deeply affected by the sufferings of the related Ponca tribe, became an early campaigner for Indian rights. It was largely because of her agitation that the Ponca chief Standing Bear—who in 1879 led a group of Poncas back from exile in Indian Territory to their traditional homeland and was summarily imprisoned in Fort Omaha, Nebraska—was brought to trial.

Susette acted as Standing Bear's interpreter before the federal court, and her eloquence helped him win a stunning victory: He was allowed to remain in Nebraska and would not be forced to return to Oklahoma. In a landmark ruling the court decided that "an Indian is a person within the meaning of the law of the United States," with a right to legal redress before the courts. Encouraged by this victory, Susette went on to campaign for full citizenship for all Native Americans, and to write a number of books detailing the injustices they were suffering.

Her half brother Francis's aims were quieter but no less crucial to his people. He decided to save what he could of the traditional culture he had known as a child. Although he qualified as a lawyer, he became an anthropologist, working for the Bureau of Indian Affairs and the Smithsonian Institution. With his mentor Alice C. Fletcher he coauthored *The Omaha Tribe,* which has been hailed as "the single most important and comprehensive study ever written about a Native American tribe."

Francis La Flesche was ideally placed to record and interpret the subtle and complex religious life of the Omaha. He knew from inside how Omaha thought was governed by a profound belief in Wakonda, the Great Spirit—the invisible life force that permeates all things, seen and unseen. The smoke of the two Sacred Pipes carried the breath of man to Wakonda.

The tribal circle or community of the Omaha consisted of two divisions, representing the Sky people and the Earth people, the original beings from whom the first Omahas were born. Each division contained five "villages," each of which bore responsibility for particular religious rites, such as those concerned with hunting buffalo.

When the whole tribe was united in the tribal circle, the unity of the people was represented by a sacred cottonwood pole known as the Venerable Man or the Sacred Pole. According to legend, the pole was cut from a miraculous shining tree sent to the people by Wakonda. The Venerable Man had a basketwork of twigs filled with feathers around his middle, and a scalp on the top for hair. The Venerable Man was regarded as a mysterious being who would provide for and protect the people—a being to whom the people prayed, and in whom was vested the power to grant the "mark of honor" to an Omaha girl. When Omaha lands were ceded to the government, the Venerable Man was allowed the same payment as a man of flesh and blood.

The Venerable Man was kept in one of three Sacred Tents, which contained all the sacred objects of the nation, such as the White Buffalo Hide. In the 1870s, as the buffalo disappeared, the Omaha appealed to Wakonda through the Venerable Man for aid. Three times the starving people laid out a thousand dollars to buy cattle to substitute for the missing buffalo, hoping to bring the buffalo back. But their appeal failed. The buffalo hunt of 1876 was the last attempted, and with the passing of the old way of life, so too passed the ceremonies of the Venerable Man, at which the sacred pole was anointed with buffalo fat mixed with a paste of red clay to celebrate success in the hunt.

Anon.
Yellow Smoke
Date unknown

Yellow Smoke (Shudenaci) was the last keeper of the Sacred Pole. He was persuaded by Francis La Flesche to lend it to the Peabody Museum for safekeeping rather than to bury it, as he intended. When Yellow Smoke revealed the sacred legend of the pole, "he continually tapped the floor with a little stick he held in his hand, marking with it the rhythm peculiar to the drumming of a man who is invoking the unseen powers during the performance of certain rites."

Ilka Hartmann
The return of the Omaha Sacred Pole
1989

The Venerable Man is diplayed to the Omaha at the annual powwow in 1989. The Sacred Pole is being held by the tribal chairman, Doran L. Morris, great-great-grandson of Yellow Smoke, the last keeper of the pole. The first of the ritual songs of the Sacred Pole translates:

The people cry aloud—
    tho ho! before thee.
Here they prepare for
    sacred rites—tho ho!
Their Sacred, Sacred
    Pole.
With reverent hands, I
    say, they touch the
    Sacred Pole before
    thee.

Francis La Flesche took part in these ceremonies as a child. As a grown man, aware that the elders of the tribe had decided that the contents of the Sacred Tents should be buried with their last guardians, he determined to save them. With the help of his father, in 1888 he persuaded Yellow Smoke, the Keeper of the Sacred Pole, to send it and associated sacred objects to Harvard's Peabody Museum.

For exactly a century, the Venerable Man of the Omaha stayed on display in a glass case in the museum—not buried, but separated from his people. Then the tribal chairman Doran L. Morris, together with Dennis Hastings, negotiated the Sacred Pole's return. The Venerable Man was welcomed back as a returning elder at a powwow on July 20, 1989.

The Sacred Pole contains the soul of the Omaha people. It was due to the forethought of Francis La Flesche, an Omaha who lived in the white man's world, that it was saved from the cultural wreck that befell the Omaha with the disappearance of the buffalo and the adjustment to reservation life. Its return in honor to its true home indicates a revival of pride in Omaha culture and identity.

This kind of cultural revival has affected many Native Americans in the decades since the 1960s. In Canada the Nuxalk Nation of Bella Coola, British Columbia, was never removed from its ancestral lands, but it still underwent catastrophic cultural change over the first decades of the twentieth century. The Nuxalk traditionally lived in extended families in large communal houses, but the old house fronts were dismantled and their carvings shipped to a museum in Ottawa, Ontario, in 1922. The Nuxalk now live in nuclear families in modern homes, and their old hunter-gatherer lifestyle has been replaced by commercial fishing and logging. Their traditional religion had a complex cycle of dramatized dances known as the Winter Ceremonial Season, which took place from November to March, in which the dancers wore elaborate wooden masks representing various mythical beings, such as Thunder. That religion has been largely replaced by Methodist Christianity.

Nevertheless, the Nuxalk remain intimately involved with their traditional beliefs, especially the legends concerning the first ancestors, who came down in animal cloaks from the House of Myths to found the first families. Each family owes its identity and knowledge to a particular ancestor, such as Whale, Bald Eagle, or Grizzly Bear. It used to be said that when a Nuxalk died, his or her spirit retraced the path of the person's ancestors down through the generations, until it reached the spot where the first ancestor descended to earth. Then it assumed the ancestor's animal cloak and rose to live in the House of Myths.

The spiritual, economic, and political hub of Nuxalk culture was the custom of the potlatch. A potlatch is a ceremonial party at which a chief proves his status by giving away valuable goods. The first potlatches were held by the mythical ancestors after they came down to earth, to demonstrate how well they had prospered in the Nuxalk

Edward Sheriff Curtis
**Clayoquot whale
ceremonial** 1916

*This Kyuquot
(Clayoquot) whaler is
performing a ritual
purification before
whaling. He bathes, rubs
his body with hemlock
sprigs, and imitates the
movements of a whale.
The Kyuquot are
culturally allied with
the Mowachaht, whose
whalers underwent very
similar rituals.*

country. Many potlatches were held in honor of deceased relatives and included rites related to the ancestral myth, staged "to wash away the grief." The Canadian government banned potlatches in 1884, because it was felt that they were keeping the native culture alive and that without them it would wither and die. Although some potlatches were still held in secret, this law did cause a critical break in the continuity of Nuxalk culture.

The publication of T. F. McIlwraith's intricately detailed two-volume study *The Bella Coola Indians* in 1948 gave the Nuxalk an authoritative record of their own traditions, gathered from the memories of Nuxalk elders in the early 1920s. This, together with the lifting of the potlatch ban three years later, provided the impetus for an active revival of Nuxalk culture, especially song and dance and the carving of ceremonial masks. Although some customs have changed or vanished, the Nuxalk remain proud of their rich and distinctive culture and will not let it disappear.

A poignant example of cultural continuity from the northwest coast is the case of the Yuquot Whalers' Shrine. The shrine at Yuquot, on the west coast of Vancouver Island, was for hundreds of years the site of sacred rites of the Mowachaht band of the Nuu-chah-nulth people, relating to the orca (killer whale) hunt. It is a shedlike wooden structure containing eighty-eight carved figures representing human beings, four carved whales, and sixteen human skulls.

In the early 1900s anthropologist Franz Boas was alerted to the shrine's existence by George Hunt, a Tlingit who made collaboration with Boas his life's work. On seeing a photograph of the shrine on an island in Jewitt Lake, flecked with sunlight through a tangle of leaves, Boas instructed Hunt to buy the shrine and its carvings for the collection of the American Museum of Natural History in New York.

Whaling had been central to life in the Nootka Sound region for at least a thousand years, and the shrine at Yuquot was controlled by chiefs descended from Chief Maquinna, who first showed it to white explorers in 1785. In rituals at the shrine, the whaling chiefs asked supernatural beings for aid in the hunt. Every aspect of preparation for the hunt had symbolic meaning; while the chief was out in his canoe, his wife remained at home, and in some profoundly mysterious sense she *became* the whale. If she remained still and quiet, the whale would be easy to catch; if she was restless, the whale would be too.

If the hunt was successful, the chief's wife welcomed the whale's carcass on the beach. The orca's spirit was believed to live in its dorsal fin, and the fin was cut off and honored with four days of ritual songs and prayers. It seems that other rituals at the shrine were intended to magically persuade this whale spirit to leave the whale's body of its own accord, causing it to die and drift ashore. The shrine at Yuquot was therefore a special and a secret place. Nobody but the hunter himself could even look at it or speak of it.

In 1983 the Mowachaht band discussed the idea of building a cultural center that would include the whalers' shrine, and in 1996 they voted to ask the American Museum of National History for the shrine back. With the help of staff at the Royal British Columbia Museum, they made a strong case for its return. The case was partly based on the way the shrine had been acquired. George Hunt had dealt with two chiefs, each of whom claimed the shrine belonged to him. They eventually agreed to sell it to him for a total of five hundred dollars on condition that he remove the shrine secretly, so that no one in the village would know it was going until it was too late.

The secrecy makes it evident that if the Mowachaht had known about the sale, they would have tried to prevent it. And whether or not Hunt was fully entitled to remove the shrine, there is no doubt that the shrine itself is an integral part of Mowachaht heritage. The case is complicated by the fact that the Mowachaht are in Canada, while the American Museum of Natural History is in the United States. This means that the informal but effective Canadian guidelines on the return of Native artifacts do not apply; nor does the Native American Grave Protection and

Repatriation Act, passed by the U.S. Congress in 1990. As of this writing, the request for return of the shrine had not been resolved.

Disputes such as this about museum artifacts, like disputes about land ownership or fishing rights, expose gaps in understanding between Indians and whites. Although many modern museums (such as the National Museum of the American Indian in Washington) are very sensitive to Native feelings about sacred objects, there is a fundamental difference in attitude. To a museum curator, the right place for objects of museum quality is in a museum, where they can be kept safe for purposes of study and education. But in a museum a sacred artifact is shorn of its cultural context and separated from the source of its power. Sending objects like the Sacred Pole of the Omaha and the Yuquot Whalers' Shrine to museums may save them from decay, but to keep them there indefinitely deprives them of meaning.

In the 1994 film *The Washing of Tears,* Jerry Jack, a Mowachaht elder, says of the shrine, "It's got to go back where it belongs. It was a part of us, the Mowachaht nation. It represented our ways. . . . It represented our strength. . . . They took away our spirituality."

The power of an object such as the Whalers' Shrine is not just in what it says about the past but in what it says about the future—about the potential for cultural revival and growth in Native societies. By 1817, when the Yuquot shrine was first fully described, the fur trade had already replaced whaling as the main activity of the Mowachaht. When George Hunt purchased the shrine for Boas in 1904, though it was still regarded as a site of great power, it was probably no longer in active use for whaling rituals. But the worldview that the shrine embodies still informs Mowachaht thought.

In June 2004 the Canadian Department of Fisheries and

Oceans attempted to capture a solitary male orca in Nootka Sound, hoping to tag it and return it to its pod or family. For nine days in a row the department's efforts were frustrated by the people of the Mowachaht/Muchalaht First Nation, who took to the waters in their canoes, luring the whale Tsux'iit (or Luna) to them with whaling songs. The Mowachaht objected to the interference, however well meant, in Tsux'iit's freedom. The idea that Tsux'iit should be captured and tagged on his dorsal fin (where traditionally the human-shaped spirit that uses the whale's body as its canoe resides) goes against the Mowachaht's deepest beliefs.

Shortly before he died in 2001, Chief Ambrose Maquinna had said he would return as an orca, to help the Mowachaht in their opposition to commercial salmon farms. Three days after Ambrose Maquinna's death, Tsux'iit arrived in Nootka Sound. To the Mowachaht, this was no coincidence. Instead, it was proof that their traditional beliefs are still a living force in the modern world.

In August 2004 the Department of Fisheries and Oceans and the Mowachaht agreed on a framework for a joint stewardship plan to protect Tsux'iit, until he chooses to reunite with his orca family. This sensitive solution incorporates Mowachaht values and meanings.

For governments to recognize the validity of Native concepts has been a slow process, but especially in Canada it has begun to pick up steam. In 1999 the Canadian government created the province of Nunavut, returning nearly one-fifth of Canada's land mass to Inuit control. In August 2003 Canada signed a new treaty with the Tli Cho (Dogrib) First Nation, giving the three thousand Tli Cho control of hunting, fishing, and industrial development in fifteen thousand square miles of territory between the Great Slave and Great Bear lakes in the Northwest Territories. The treaty was signed in a grade-school gymnasium. Jean Chrétien, the

Canadian prime minister, said, "What we see today is that in spite of the evolution of society, you have kept your culture and pride. This is the glory of Canada—we can be what we are and at the same time be part of the greater Canada." Tli Cho elder Alexis Arrowmaker said simply, "The promises that were made, they have been fulfilled. Whatever we asked for, they gave us."

New treaties that try to repair the damage done by earlier treaties, which effectively stole Native people's land from them, are tremendously important. Under the 2003 treaty with the Tli Cho, the federal government retains its powers of law enforcement, the Northwest Territories continue to administer services such as health and education, and the Tli Cho win stewardship of the land, financial compensation, and self-government in the matters most important to them. Here at last is a treaty no one need feel ashamed of.

Among the Lakota, the loss of the sacred Black Hills in 1877 was felt as a cultural wound. As early as 1891—the year after the massacre at Wounded Knee—three hundred

Lakota men calling themselves the Oglala Council established monthly meetings to work out a way of reclaiming the Black Hills. By the time the Lakota were legally able to file a claim for the Black Hills, in 1923, the traditionalists who wanted the land back were outnumbered by progressives who preferred to settle for the "best price" they could negotiate. However, the case proceeded so slowly that by the time it was settled, in June 1980, the traditionalists were once more in the majority. The Oglala Sioux tribal council voted to have nothing to do with the compensation offered, and other Lakota tribal councils followed suit. Today over $500 million is sitting unclaimed in the United States Treasury because, as Crazy Horse said, "One does not sell the earth upon which the people walk."

In Taos Pueblo in New Mexico, an Indian nation still lives in cultural continuity with the ancient past. As a settled agricultural community, Taos dates back at least a thousand years. In 1992 the Pueblo was declared a World Heritage Site. One Taos Pueblo man said in 1970:

> We have lived upon this land from days beyond history's records, far past any living memory, deep into the time of legend. The story of my people and the story of this place are one single story. No man can think of us without thinking of this place. We are always joined together.

Probably as a reaction to Spanish attempts to suppress traditional religion in the seventeenth century, Taos—like other Pueblo nations—has maintained a strong commitment to secrecy about religious and cultural matters. However, in the twentieth century the Taos had to lift the curtain on their religious life during their campaign to regain control of their most important sacred site—Blue Lake, a high mountain lake that is the source of the village water supply. Taos governor Severino Martinez said in

1961, "Religion is the most important thing in a person's life because without religion, without a prayer, no individual can exist."

In 1906 the area around Blue Lake was designated a national forest, and the Taos immediately began to campaign for its return. In 1926 the U.S. government made them an offer of financial compensation, which was refused. Only in 1940 were the Taos granted a permit to conduct religious ceremonies at the lake, but this was unsatisfactory from their point of view because of the high degree of secrecy required for religious activities.

The dispute over Blue Lake was the kind of problem that the federal Indian Claims Commission, set up in 1946, was intended to settle, and in 1951 the Taos filed their claim. Although the Commission eventually ruled in their favor, it had no authority to return land, only to offer financial compensation, which the Taos refused with the words "We will not sell our religion—our life."

Two attempts in the 1960s to return Blue Lake to the Taos came to nothing. The Taos tried again in 1970, with an appeal to Congress that read in part:

> We testify in good faith that our religious needs require the entire watershed to be maintained intact as an ecological unit. . . . The entire watershed is permeated with holy places and shrines used regularly by our Indian people; there is no place that does not have religious significance to us.

Ceremonial water vase 19th century

This typical piece of pueblo pottery is of Sia manufacture.

Finally, in 1970 Congress returned forty-eight thousand acres of Carson National Forest to the Taos, including Blue Lake. The cacique (priest-chief) of Taos, Juan de Jesus Romero, then ninety years old, told an audience at the White House that his prayers at Blue Lake were for "all America and its people . . . to protect the life and to protect what this America is, really beautiful, peace, honesty, truth, understanding, consideration."

Ilka Hartmann
The Long Walk for Survival 1980

Native Americans and their supporters (note, for instance, a Japanese Buddhist in the knitted cap) prepare food during the Long Walk for Survival, from Alcatraz Island to Washington. The walkers called for an end to nuclear development and uranium mining; more than 50% of all uranium mining in the United States is on Indian land.

Mountain Lake, a Taos Pueblo elder, said much the same to the psychologist Carl Jung:

> We are the people who live on the roof of the world, we are the sons of the Sun who is our father. We help him daily to rise and to cross the sky. We do this not only for ourselves, but for the Americans also. Therefore they should not interfere with our religion.

The intense traditionalism of Taos life, which means that even today no electricity or running water is allowed within the pueblo walls, is remarkable in twenty-first-century America. But across Native America, traditional ways of thinking, behaving, and believing are being retrieved and revalidated by Indians who believe there is both access to the past and hope for the future in the old wisdom of their peoples.

In contrast to the suppression of Native traditions in the

past, modern laws provide a nurturing environment for this kind of cultural revival. In the United States the 1973 American Indian Freedom of Religion Act protects traditional Indian religion under the First Amendment. The 1975 Indian Self-Determination and Educational Assistance Act gives Indian nations control over the schooling of their children. And the 1990 Native American Languages Act safeguards the languages previous generations of Indian children were beaten for speaking at white-run schools.

Alongside the revival of traditional culture there is also increasing assimilation into the mainstream culture. Even traditionalists do not as a rule live a life outside the modern world. They dwell in modern houses, wear modern clothes, hold down a wide range of jobs, drive trucks and cars, own televisions, shop at supermarkets. Mohawk steelworkers, famed for their fearlessness, played a key role both in building the World Trade Center in New York and in cleaning up the dangerous site after the attack of 9/11.

Thousands of Native Americans fought with the U.S. armed forces in World War I—though, since they were not American citizens, they were not eligible for the draft. It was partly in recognition of this service that all Native Americans were granted American citizenship in 1924—a gift not welcomed by all, as peoples such as the Iroquois jealously guarded their status as sovereign independent nations.

When World War II came, twenty-five thousand Native Americans were drafted. For warrior nations like the Lakota, this was the first opportunity since the Indian wars to explore their heritage of individual courage in battle. Many Lakotas distinguished themselves undertaking hazardous reconnaissance missions in the infantry. There was also a unit of Lakota code talkers in the South Pacific, who communicated vital information in an unbreakable Lakota code, similar to that used by the better-known Navajo code talkers. The American Legion and Veterans of Foreign Wars are prestigious organizations among today's Lakota.

The key for the First Nations has been to find their own way forward rather than follow a predetermined path. "Self-determination for Native Americans" is now the official policy of the U.S. government after centuries in which even those who sympathized with the Indians thought the only way forward was to turn them into whites.

Massachusetts Senator Henry Dawes was the architect of the General Allotment Act of 1887, which broke up the communal land of reservations into individual plots of 160 acres and returned the "surplus" land left over to the public domain. This misguided policy ("a bureaucratic genocide," according to Charlotte Black Elk, a Lakota) was intended to destroy the traditional social structures of Native American societies, which emphasized sharing wealth rather than storing it up for oneself. As Dawes said, the Indians had "no selfishness, which is at the bottom of civilization."

The 1934 Indian Reorganization Act—cornerstone of the so-called Indian New Deal—was rejected by 77 nations, including the Iroquois Six Nations, the Five Civilized Tribes, and the Navajo. To the 181 nations who accepted it, the act gave self-government, but on alien terms. It required each nation to hold competitive elections for political office, contrary to the Indian way of electing by consensus, and thus laid the groundwork for bitter splits and disputes of a kind many nations had never experienced before.

As late as the 1950s, the official policy of "termination" was intended to destroy the reservation system and integrate the First Nations fully into the mainstream of society by cutting all federal ties to Indian communities. The obliteration of traditional Native values and concerns was seen as a positive step forward to "civilization."

"Termination" was slowed down and eventually halted as a result of political pressure from the National Congress of

American Indians, formed in 1944 as the first truly national pan-Indian body since Tecumseh tried to unite the nations in 1810. This first tentative move toward exercising political muscle was rapidly overtaken by the younger, more radical voices of the National Indian Youth Council, who derided the members of the National Congress as "Uncle Tomahawks," a reference to the elderly slave in the novel *Uncle Tom's Cabin*.

The American Indian Movement (AIM) was founded in 1968 by Anishinaabes, including George Mitchell, Dennis Banks, and Mary Jane Wilson. Direct action and civil disobedience at fish-ins in the northwest states of Oregon, Washington, and Idaho provided a first taste of the kind of provocative publicity stunts that would be the group's trademark. AIM "reclaimed" Alcatraz, marched to Washington on "the Trail of Broken Treaties," and, on February

Ilka Hartmann
Dennis Banks 1976

The AIM founder is speaking at a San Francisco rally fighting his extradition to South Dakota. Banks believed that, "If we Native People are to survive as a cultural species, then we must follow the way of our ancestors."

27, 1973, occupied the site of the massacre of Wounded
Knee, for a tense siege that lasted seventy-one days.

The Lakota medicine man Leonard Crow Dog, a key
figure in the revival of the Lakota Sun Dance, was the last
"hostile" to be removed from Wounded Knee by the FBI.
He wrote:

> We never got our Black Hills back, the Treaty of Fort
> Laramie was not honored, nor did the government rec-
> ognize us as an independent nation. And yet I think that
> this was the greatest moment in my life and that our
> seventy-one-day stand was the greatest deed done by
> Native Americans in this century.

The activists of AIM were to pay a high price for their
radical politics. As the first Native people to stand up
aggressively for Indian rights since the days of Crazy Horse
and Sitting Bull, they were treated as enemies of the state.
The FBI collaborated in what the U.S. Commission on Civil

Rights was to call a "reign of terror" on the Lakota Pine Ridge Reservation. More than sixty AIM members were murdered in the three years following the siege at Wounded Knee, and there were violent attacks on many more. Leaders such as Dennis Banks, Russell Means, and Leonard Crow Dog were harassed with criminal charges; one, Leonard Peltier, remains in jail at this writing for the double murder of two FBI agents in a firefight at Oglala in 1975, despite the admitted fact that evidence against him was fabricated.

No one would deny the many problems facing Native American communities today, including alcoholism, depression, and discrimination. Some nations, such as the Akimel O'odham, have suffered serious health problems adjusting to a less active lifestyle and a rich western diet. The Akimel O'odham were genetically adapted to a desert environment in which food and water were both in short supply; today more than half of all adults develop diabetes at the young average age of thirty-six.

Problems like widespread alcoholism and depression developed out of a sense of hopelessness and helplessness. The answer to them has been to reclaim control. Native Americans today are determined to preserve their traditional culture, to develop their communities in accordance with their traditional values, to stand up for their rights, and to determine their own futures.

One unexpected development has been the billions of dollars raised by casinos on Indian reservations, established by the Indian Gaming Regulatory Act of 1988. The hard-core gambling that goes in such establishments has none of the religious context, the fun, or the laughter of traditional Indian gambling, and many Native Americans object to the greed and commercialism it fosters. But the money flowing in from the casinos has revolutionized the finances of many of the First Nations.

The Mashantucket Pequot Tribal Nation of Connecticut offers the most spectacular example of this gambling-led revival of fortunes. In the early seventeenth century they numbered around eight thousand people, with 250 square miles of territory they had occupied for thousands of years. In 1634 they were devastated by a smallpox epidemic. The Pequot War of 1636–38—the first major conflict between Europeans and Native Americans—nearly destroyed them.

In 1975 the Mashantucket Pequot reservation contained 175 acres (down from 1,737 acres in 1732), with just nine full-time residents; there were fifty-five people on the tribal membership rolls. In 1976, after intensive lobbying from the Nation, an 1856 land sale was declared illegal, and the size of the reservation was increased to 1,250 acres. Tribal members began returning to the reservation, and the Nation opened first a restaurant, then a bingo hall, and then, in 1992, the Foxwoods Resort Casino. The Mashantucket Pequot are now in a position to contribute at least a million dollars a year in gambling profits to aid urban problem areas in the state of Connecticut.

This is not just—or even mainly—a story about poor people getting rich. Much of the profit from the Foxwoods Casino has been spent on the Mashantucket Pequot Museum and Research Center, a lavish facility celebrating the cultural heritage of Native Americans in general and the Pequot in particular. At the museum, documentary films are shown. In one of them a fourteen-year-old tribal member, Tabitha Cooper, expresses in her hopes for the future a new-found optimism and drive: "I'm going straight through college to get every kind of degree I can. And I want to be a lawyer."

The Mashantucket Pequot have used their money to celebrate the past, to help in the present, and to plan for the future. And if any young Native American today wants to become a lawyer, he or she can do so—unlike Ely S. Parker,

who was prevented from practicing law at the New York bar because he was an Indian.

No neat ending can give a true picture of the First Nations today. They contain probably three million individuals, with different ideas, beliefs, and goals. But it can be said for sure that the Native Americans are not planning to "vanish" anytime soon.

The Lakota medicine man Archie Fire Lame Deer says that the First Nations are "caretakers of the Earth." Long may they remain so. In the words of a Californian prayer to the seven gods of the Yokuts:

> Do you see me!
> Do you help me!
> My words are tied in one
> With the great mountains,
> With the great rocks,
> With the great trees,
> In one with my body
> And my heart.
> Do you all help me
> With supernatural power,
> And you, day,
> And you, night!
> All of you see me
> One with this world!

SOURCE NOTES

These notes are intended to enable readers to refer easily to the sources of quotes in the text; references (with abbreviated titles and page numbers) are to the works listed in the Bibliography under "General" or under individual chapters. Titles of works are given in the first instance only, except where it is necessary to distinguish between several works by the same author.

ix "The power of the world": Neihardt, *Black Elk Speaks* 194; "from savagery": Powell, *23rd Annual Report of the BAE* xxi; "a young girl": Reichard, *Navaho Religion* 46; **x** "The thought": Curtis, *The North American Indian:The Complete Portfolios* 36; **xiii** "I am from the Sand Clan": Moquin & Van Doren, *Great Documents* 336; "And I saw": Neihardt, 43; **1** "My children": Mooney, *The Ghost-Dance Religion* 961; **2** "A fat paunch": Fitzhugh & Ward, *Vikings* 203; "a large number of the natives": Fitzhugh & Ward, 221; **3** "God created this Indian country": Moquin & Van Doren, *Great Documents* 297; **4** "The earth is part of my body": Josephy, *The Nez Perce Indians* 503; **5** "The Apaches and their homes": Barrett, *Geronimo* 69; **7** "I am king in my land": Josephy, *500 Nations* 143; "It was very fortunate": Josephy, *500 Nations* 146; **12** "count the stars in the sky": Josephy, *500 Nations* 204; **14** "Brothers, you see this vast country": Miller, *From the Heart* 71; "My heart breaks": Miller, 75; **15** "We bury them from sight": Armstrong, *I Have Spoken* 10; "thinking will replace violence": Richter, *The Ordeal of the Longhouse* 32; **17** "There was a time": Moquin & Van Doren, 31; **19** "My cause will not die": Miller, 95; "to punish the delinquents": Wilson, *The Earth Shall Weep* 127; "You will do well to inoculate": Miller, 95; **20** "The Ottawas were greatly reduced": Miller, 96; "The land on which you are": Wilson, 126; **21** "roaring like the falls": Sugden, *Tecumseh* 116; "Who is this pretended prophet": Sugden, 124; **23** "The Americans I did not make": Miller, 187; "The religion which I have established": Drake, *The Life of Tecumseh* 108; **25** "The Great Spirit": Sugden, 18; "the Wellington of the Indians": Sugden, 308; "the bravest man": Sugden, 377; **26** "Tecumseh's appearance": Sugden, 300; "With these hands": Sugden, 72; **27** "I am alone": Sugden, 72; "My heart is a stone": Philip, *In a Sacred Manner I Live* 72; **28** "be all of one mind": Sugden,187; "is for all the red men to unite": Moquin & Van Doren, 134; **29** "the earth was the most proper place": Sugden, 198; "I do not see how we can remain at peace": Sugden, 199; **30** "Well, as the Great Chief": Sugden, 202; "one of those uncommon geniuses": Sugden, 215; "nor should his white brothers complain": Sugden, 223; **31** "Brothers, the Great Spirit is angry": Sugden, 255; **32** "Had I been at home": Sugden, 270; "speak loud and look big": Sugden, 282; "Ho-yo-o-e!": Sugden, 300; **33** "to an extensive tract of land": Sugden, 311; **34** "Never did Tecumseh shine": Sugden, 334; "Begone!": Sugden, 337;

"He was dressed": Sugden, 371; **35** "a fat animal": Sugden, 359; "Listen, Father!": Sugden, 359-360; **39** "I saw a trail": Miller, 147; **40** "to set upon": Mooney, *Myths of the Cherokee* 32; "continue the guarantee": Mooney, *Myths* 81; **41** "The Cherokees had broken the road": Mooney, *Myths* 88; "the maddened followers": Mooney, *Myths* 88; "We can never forget": Ehle, *Trail of Tears* 294; **42** "their bees, their orchards": Mooney, *Myths* 88; **43** "made herself a *squaw*": Ehle, 189; "has been increasing": Perdue & Green, *The Cherokee Removal* 35; **44** "The African slaves": Perdue & Green, 35; **45** "I thought that would be like catching a wild animal": Debo, *A History of the Indians of the United States* 112; "Within a few months": Mooney, *Myths* 110; **47** "It is true we Govern ourselves": Perdue & Green, 65; **48** "It is the fixed and unalterable determination": Mooney, *Myths* 115; **49** "No Indian or descendant of any Indian": Perdue & Green, 65; "All I ask in this creation": Ehle, 213; "The American Indians": Perdue & Green, 96; **51** "You asked us to throw off the hunter and warrior state": Ehle, 254; "ignorant and barbarous": Perdue & Green, 112; "somewhat like human beings": Perdue & Green, 15; "It gives me pleasure": Perdue & Green, 119; "Well, it seems": Mooney, *Myths* 163; **52** "The weather was excessively cold": Perdue & Green, 86; **53** "Our Nation is crumbling": Ehle, 271; **54** "I have signed my death warrant": Ehle, 295; "to legislate the Indians off the land": Perdue & Green, 149; "If I had known that Jackson would drive us from our homes": Mooney, *Myths* 126; **55** "The Cherokee are a peaceable, harmless people": Mooney, *Myths* 126; "The whole scene": Ehle, 302; "I fought through the Civil War": Mooney, *Myths* 130; **56** "When the soldiers came": Perdue & Green, 169; **61** "My people, we were born in this country": Riddle, *Indian History of the Modoc War* 19; "people of a tractable, free, and loving nature": Debo, 33; "When they first came": Godard, *Hupa Texts* 201; **62** "It was of no infrequent occurrence": Debo, 159; "Abducting Indian children": Debo, 165; **63** "You will eat clover": Curtin, *Creation Myths* 483; **64** "They had resolved": Curtin, 517; **65** "At Millville": Curtin, 518; "the last wild Indian": Kroeber, *Ishi in Two Worlds* 237; "He was the most patient man": Kroeber, 229; **66** "I thought if we killed all the white men": Quinn, *Hell with the Fire Out,* 26; **68** "a goneness in my heart": Quinn, 10; "would get very excited": Quinn, 75; **69** "I don't know any other country": Quinn, 102; "We have made a mistake": Quinn, 75; "I want war": Quinn, 75; **70** "Fog! Fog!": Mooney, *Ghost-Dance*: 1054; "like a black ocean": Quinn, 72; **71** "We can kill all the white men": Quinn, 83; "This tribe was living in peace": Quinn, 83; "Nobody will every want these rocks": Quinn, 101; **72** "I do not want to fight": Quinn, 104; "Tell Old Man Meacham": Quinn, 105; "You may be a widow tonight": Quinn, 117; **73** "My heart tells me": Riddle, 161; **74** "half-naked children": Quinn, 162; **75** "I am on the edge of my grave": Miller, 314; **77** "My ancestors were glad": McWhorter, *Yellow Wolf* 35; **79** "kind to strangers": Josephy, *Nez Perce* 140; **80** "he had received the wyakin": Josephy, *Nez Perce* 217; **81** "the influence of the gospel": Josephy, *Nez Perce* 223; "If we make a treaty": Josephy, *Nez Perce* 322; "I hear what this earth says": Josephy, *Nez Perce* 325; **82** "My people, what have you done?": Josephy, *Nez Perce* 328; "peace, plows, and schools": Josephy, *Nez Perce:* 320; **83** "What a miracle": Josephy, *Nez Perce* 408; "The white men dig up and take the gold": Josephy, *Nez Perce* 405; **84** "You are the chief": Moquin & Van Doren, 240; **85** "Twenty times over": Brown, *Bury My Heart at Wounded Knee* 321; "Who can tell me what I must do": McWhorter,

Yellow Wolf 40; **86** "Bullets from everywhere!": McWhorter, *Yellow Wolf* 212; **88** "I am tired": Beal, *I Will Fight No More Forever* 229; "I rose up and ran up the creek": McWhorter, *Hear Me, My Chiefs* 385; **91** "Young men, help me": Vestal, *Sitting Bull* 97; "I will remain": Utley, *The Lance and the Shield* 206; **95** "We have waited a long time": Meyer, *History of the Santee Sioux* 114; "the whites would take": Meyer, 115; **96** "So far as I am concerned": Meyer, 114; "Kill one—two—ten": Wilson, 271; "White men with guns": Wilson, 271; "They are poor": Namias, *White Captives* 224; "savage murderers": Namias, 232; **97** "You hung him yesterday": Meyer, 130; **98** "Damn any man": Wilson, 273; **99** "At dawn": Hyde, *Life of George Bent* 151; "the worst night": Hyde, 157; **100** "Nothing lives long": Hyde, 155; "For my part": Brown, 130; **102** "I mean to keep this land": Brown, 144; **103** "We are on the mountains": Brown, 145; "It is all lies": Larson, *Red Cloud* 133; "All I want": Moquin & Van Doren, 212; **104** "the heart of everything": Wilson, 281; "Many soldiers": Brown, 288; **105** "When the last soldier": Dixon, *The Vanishing Race* 176; **107** "He laid down his ax": Mooney *Ghost-Dance*, 772; "President of the West": Hittman, *Wovoka* 153; **108** "gave him the power to destroy this world": Hittman, 235; **109** "the whole world and all that was wonderful": Neihardt, 235; "a beautiful land": Neihardt, 242; **110** "There must be peace": Hittman, 232; "Yes, take it off": Mooney, *Ghost-Dance* 878; **111** "I love my children": Mooney, *Ghost-Dance* 1065; **113** "My friend, I am old": Miller, 186; "The American government": Moquin & Van Doren, 190; **114** "I learn from Lieutenant J. J. Jackson": Barrett, *Geronimo* 35; **115** "As we were feasting there": De Mallie, *The Sixth Grandfather* 276; **116** "where they killed Jesus": De Mallie, 10; **117** "Those of use here on earth": De Mallie, 19; "As I sit here": Neihardt, xvii; "What I know": Neihardt, xviii; "a North American bible": Vine Deloria in Neihardt, xiii; **118** "future generations of the Oglalas": Walker, *Lakota Belief and Ritual:* 47; **119** "the Village": Fletcher & La Flesche, *The Omaha Tribe* 633; "I was always sure": Fletcher & La Flesche, 634; **120** "and sees his only chance": Fletcher & La Flesche, 638; "an Indian is a person": Hoxie, *Encyclopedia of the North American Indians* 427; "the single most important and comprehensive study": Robin Ridington in Fletcher & La Flesche, 1; **122** "The people cry aloud": Fletcher & La Flesche, 234; **124** "to wash away the grief": Sturtevant *Handbook of North American Indians vol. 7,* 333; **127** "It's got to go back where it belongs": Jonaitis, *The Yuquot Whalers' Shrine* 45; **129** "What we see today": David Usborne, "Canadian Indians Given Huge Area in Self-Rule Deal," *The Independent* August 27, 2003; "The promises that were made": Usborne, as p.129; **130** "One does not sell the earth": Miller, 244; "We have lived upon this land": Miller, 269; "Religion is the most important thing": Debo, 419; "We will not sell our religion": Debo, 419; **131** "We testify in good faith": Moquin & Van Doren, 386-387; "all America and its people": Josephy, Nagel, & Johnson, *Red Power* 149; **132** "We are the people": Nabokov, *Native American Testimony* 41; **134** "a bureaucratic genocide": Wilson, 308; "no selfishness": Wilson, 300; **135** "If we Native People": Josephy, Nagel, & Johnson, 62; **136** "We never got our Black Hills back": Crow Dog & Erdoes, *Crow Dog* 209; **138** "I'm going straight through college": www.pequotmuseum.org; **139** "caretakers of the earth": Lame Deer & Erdoes, *Gift of Power* 254; **139** "Do you see me!": Kroeber, *Handbook of the Indians of California* 511.

BIBLIOGRAPHY

This bibliography lists the major works I have relied on in writing this book, but is by no means a complete list of works consulted.

GENERAL

Bruchac, Joseph. *Lasting Echoes: An Oral History of Native American People.* San Diego: Silver Whistle, 1997.
Curtis, Edward Sheriff. *The North American Indian.* Vols. 1–5, Cambridge, Mass.: The University Press. Vols. 6–20, Norwood, Conn.: Plimpton Press. 1907–30.
———. *The North American Indian: The Complete Portfolios.* Köln: Taschen, 1997.
Debo, Angie. *A History of the Indians of the United States.* Norman, Okla.: University of Oklahoma Press, 1973.
Deloria, Vine, Jr. *Red Earth, White Lies: Native Americans and the Myth of Scientific Fact.* Golden, Colo.: Fulcrum Publishing, 1997.
Hoxie, Frederick, ed. *Encyclopedia of North American Indians.* Boston: Houghton Mifflin, 1996.
———, and Peter Iverson, eds. *Indians in American History: An Introduction.* Wheeling, Ill.: Harlan Davidson, Inc., 1998.
Josephy, Alvin M., Jr. *500 Nations: An Illustrated History of North American Indians.* New York: Alfred A. Knopf, 1994.
Miller, Lee, ed. *From the Heart: Voices of the American Indian.* New York: Alfred A. Knopf, 1995.
Mooney, James. *The Ghost-Dance Religion and Wounded Knee.* New York: Dover Publications, 1973; reprint of 1896 edition.
Moquin, Wayne, with Charles Van Doren, eds.. *Great Documents in American Indian History.* New York: Da Capo Press, *1995.*
Nabokov, Peter, ed. *Native American Testimony: A Chronicle of Indian-White Relations from Prophecy to the Present, 1492–1992.* New York: Viking Penguin, 1991.
Philip, Neil. *In a Sacred Manner I Live: Native American Wisdom.* New York: Clarion, 1997.
Sturtevant, William C., ed. *Handbook of North American Indians.* Vol. 9: *History of Indian-White Relations.* Wilcomb E. Washburn, volume editor.
Taylor, Colin F., ed. *The Native Americans: The Indigenous People of North America.* San Diego: Thunder Bay, 1999.
Wilson, James. *The Earth Shall Weep: A History of Native America.* New York: Atlantic Monthly, 1999.

INTRODUCTION

Coolidge, Dane, and Mary Roberts Coolidge. *The Last of the Seris.* New York: E. P. Dutton, 1939.
Kluckhohn, Clyde, and Dorothea Leighton. *The Navaho.* Cambridge: Harvard University Press, 1948.
Mails, Thomas E. *The Hopi Survival Kit.* New York: Penguin Compass, 1997.
Neihardt, John G. *Black Elk Speaks: Being the Life Story of a Holy Man of the Oglala Sioux.* Lincoln, Neb.: University of Nebraska Press, 1979; reprint of 1932 edition.
Powell, J. W. "Report of the Director," in *23rd Annual Report of the Bureau of American Ethnology.* Washington: Government Printing Office, 1904.
Reichard, Gladys A. *Navaho Religion: A Study of Symbolism.* Princeton, N. J.: Princeton University Press, 1990; reprint of 1950 edition.
Waters, Frank. *Book of the Hopi.* New York: Viking, 1963.

CHAPTER ONE

Fitzhugh, William, and Elisabeth I. Ward, eds. *Vikings: The North Atlantic Saga.* Washington D.C.: Smithsonian Institution, 2000.
Jennings, Francis. *The Ambiguous Iroquois Empire: The Covenant Chain Confederation of Idina Tribe with English Colonies.* New York: W. W. Norton, 1990.
———. *The Founders of America: From the Earliest Migrations to the Present.* New York: W. W. Norton, 1994.
———. *The Invasion of America: Indians, Colonialism, and the Cant of Conquest.* New York: W. W. Norton, 1976.
Menzies, Gavin. *1421: The Year the Chinese Discovered America.* New York: William Morrow, 2003.
Milton, Giles. *Big Chief Elizabeth: The Adventures and Fate of the First English Colonists in America.* New York: Farrar, Straus and Giroux, 2000.
Richter, Daniel K. *The Ordeal of the Longhouse.* Chapel Hill, N.C.: University of North Carolina Press, 1993.
Sando, Joe S. *Pueblo Nations: Eight Centuries of Pueblo Indian History.* Santa Fe, N.M.: Clear Light Publishers, 1992.
Sturtevant, William C., ed. Ortiz, Alfonso. *Handbook of North American Indians.* Vol. 9: *Southwest.* Alfonso Ortiz, volume editor. Washington, D.C.: Smithsonian Institution, 1979.
———. *Handbook of North American Indians.* Vol. 15: *Northeast.* Bruce G. Trigger, volume editor. Washington, D.C.: Smithsonian Insitution, 1978.
Wright, Ronald. *Stolen Continents: The "New World" Through Indian Eyes.* Boston: Houghton Mifflin, 1992.

CHAPTER TWO

Dowd, Gregory Evans. *A Spirited Resistance: The North American Indian Struggle for Unity, 1745–1815.* Baltimore: Johns Hopkins University Press, 1992.
Drake, Benjamin. *The Life of Tecumseh and His Brother the Prophet: Historical Sketches of the Shawnee Indians.* Honolulu: University Press of the Pacific, 2002; reprint of 1841 edition.
Edmunds, R. David. *The Shawnee Prophet.* Lincoln, Neb.: University of Nebraska Press, 1983.
Sugden, John. *Tecumseh: A Life.* New York: Henry Holt, 1998.
Warren, William W. *A History of the Ojibway People.* St. Paul, Minn.: Minnesota Historical Society Press, 1984; reprint of 1885 edition.

CHAPTER THREE

Ehle, John. *Trail of Tears: The Rise and Fall of the Cherokee Nation.* New York: Doubleday Anchor Books, 1988.
Littlefield, Daniel F., and James W. Parins. *Native American Writing in the Southeast: An Anthology, 1875–1935.* Jackson, Miss.: University Press of Mississippi, 1995.
McLoughlin, William G. *After the Trail of Tears: The Cherokees' Struggle for Sovereignty, 1839–1880.* Chapel Hill, N.C.: University of North Carolina Press, 1993.
Mooney, James. *Myths of the Cherokee.* New York: Dover Publications, 1995; reprint of 1900 edition.
———. *The Swimmer Manuscript: Cherokee Sacred Formulas and Medicinal Prescriptions.* Frans M. Obrechts, ed.. Washington, D.C.: Smithsonian Institution, 1932.
Perdue, Theda. *Slavery and the Evolution of Cherokee Society, 1540–1866.* Knoxville, Tenn.: University of Tennessee Press, 1979.
———, ed. *Nations Remembered: An Oral History of the Cherokees, Chickasaws, Choctaws, Creeks, and Seminoles in Oklahoma, 1865–1907.* Norman, Okla.: University of Oklahoma Press, 1993; reprint of 1980 edition.
———, and Michael D. Green, eds. *The Cherokee Removal: A Brief History with Documents.* Boston and New York: Bedford Books of St. Martin's Press, 1995.
Swanton, John R. *The Indians of the Southeastern United States.* Washington, D.C.: Smithsonian Insitution, 1946.

CHAPTER FOUR

Curtin, Jeremiah. *Creation Myths of Primitive America in Relation to the Religious History and Mental Development of Mankind.* New York: Benjamin Blom, 1968; reprint of 1899 edition.
———. *Myths of the Modocs.* New York: Benjamin Blom, 1971; reprint of 1912 edition.
Godard, Pliny Earle. *Hupa Texts.* Berkeley, Calif.: The University Press, 1904.
Sturtevant, William C., ed. *Handbook of North American Indians.* Vol. 8: *California.* Robert F. Heizer, volume editor. Washington, D.C.: Smithsonian Institution, 1978.
Kroeber, Alfred. L. *Handbook of the Indians of California.* New York: Dover Publications, 1976; reprint of 1925 edition.
Quinn, Arthur. *Hell with the Fire Out: A History of the Modoc War.* Boston: Faber & Faber, 1997.
Riddle, Jeff C. *The Indian History of the Modoc War.* San Jose, Calif.: Urion Press, 1974; reprint of 1914 edition.

CHAPTER FIVE

Beal, Merrill D. *"I Will Fight No More Forever": Chief Joseph and the Nez Perce War.* Seattle, Wash.: University of Washington Press, 1963.
Howard, Helen Addison. *Saga of Chief Joseph.* Lincoln, Neb.: University of Nebraska Press, 1978; reprint of 1971 edition.
Josephy, Alvin M., Jr. *The Nez Perce Indians and the Opening of the Northwest.* Boston: Houghton Mifflin, 1997; reprint of 1965 edition.
McWhorter, L. V. *Hear Me, My Chiefs! Nez Perce History and Legend.* Caldwell, Idaho: The Caxton Printers, Ltd., 1983; reprint of 1952 edition.
———. *Yellow Wolf: His Own Story.* Caldwell, Idaho: The Caxton Printers, Ltd., 1940.
Splawn, A. J. *Ka-Mi-Akin, The Last Hero of the Yakimas.* Portland, Ore.: Privately printed, 1917.
Sturtevant, William C., ed. *Handbook of North American Indian.* Vol. 12: *Plateau.* Deward E. Walker, Jr., volume editor. Washington, D.C.: Smithsonian Institution, 1998.

CHAPTER SIX

Brown, Dee. *Bury My Heart at Wounded Knee: An Indian History of the American West.* New York: Henry Holt, 2001.
Dixon, Joseph K. *The Vanishing Race: The Last Great Indian Council.* New York: Bonanza Books, n.d.; reprint of 1913 edition.
Hittman, Michael. *Wovoka and the Ghost Dance.* Lincoln, Neb.: University of Nebraska Press, 1997.
Hyde, George E. *Life of George Bent, Written from His Letters.* Norman, Okla.: University of Oklahoma Press, 1968.
———. *Red Cloud's Folk: A History of the Oglala Sioux Indians.* Norman, Okla.: University of Oklahoma Press, 1937.
Larson, Robert W. *Red Cloud: Warrior-Statesman of the Lakota Sioux.* Norman, Okla.: University of Oklahoma Press, 1997.
Meyer, Roy W. *History of the Santee Sioux: United States Indian Policy on Trial.* Rev. ed. Lincoln, Neb.: University of Nebraska Press, 1993.
Namias, June. *White Captives: Gender and Ethnicity on the American Frontier.* Chapel Hill, N.C.: The University of North Carolina Press, 1993.
Neihardt, John G. *When the Tree Flowered: The Story of Eagle Voice, a Sioux Indian.* Lincoln, Neb.: University of Nebraska Press, 1991; reprint of 1951 edition.
Paul, R. Eli, ed. *Autobiography of Red Cloud, War Leader of the Oglalas.* Helena, Mont.: Montana Historical Society Press, 1997.
Sandoz, Mari. *Crazy Horse, the Strange Man of the Oglalas: A Biography.* Lincoln, Neb.: University of Nebraska Press, 1992; reprint of 1942 edition.
Standing Bear, Luther. *My People, the Sioux.* Lincoln, Neb.: University of Nebraska Press, 1975; reprint of 1928 edition.

Sturtevant, William C, ed. *Handbook of North American Indians*. Vol. 13: *Plains*. Raymond J. DeMallie, volume editor. Washington, D.C.: Smithsonian Institution, 2001.

Taylor, Colin F. *The Plains Indians: A Cultural and Historical View of the North American Plains Tribes of the Pre-Reservation Period*. London: Tiger Books International, 1997.

Utley, Robert M. *The Lance and the Shield: The Life and Times of Sitting Bull*. New York: Henry Holt, 1993.

Vestal, Stanley. *Sitting Bull: Champion of the Sioux*. Norman, Okla.: University of Oklahoma Press, 1989; reprint of 1957 edition.

———. *Warpath: The True Story of the Fighting Sioux, Told in a Biography of Chief White Bull*. Lincoln, Neb.: University of Nebraska Press, 1984; reprint of 1962 edition.

CHAPTER SEVEN

Barrett, S. M., ed. *Geronimo: His Own Story*. New York: E. P. Dutton, 1970.

Brown, Joseph Epes, ed. *The Sacred Pipe: Black Elk's Account of the Seven Rites of the Oglala Sioux*. Norman, Okla.: University of Oklahoma Press, 1989; reprint of 1953 edition.

Cash, Joseph H., and Herbert T. Hoover, eds. *To Be an Indian: An Oral History*. New edition. St. Paul, Minn.: Minnesota Historical Society Press, 1995.

Crow Dog, Leonard, and Richard Erdoes. *Crow Dog: Four Generations of Sioux Medicine Men*. New York: HarperCollins, 1995.

Deloria, Vine, Jr. *Custer Died for Your Sins: An Indian Manifesto*. New edition. Norman, Okla.: University of Oklahoma Press, 1988.

De Mallie, Raymond J., ed. *The Sixth Grandfather: Black Elk's Teachings Given to John G. Neihardt*. Lincoln, Neb.: University of Nebraska Press, 1984.

Fletcher, Alice C., and Francis La Flesche. *The Omaha Tribe*. Lincoln, Neb.: University of Nebraska Press, 1992; reprint of 1911 edition.

Jonaitis, Aldona. *The Yuquot Whalers' Shrine*. Seattle, Wash.: University of Washington Press, 1999.

Josephy, Alvin M., Jr., Joane Nagel, and Troy Johnson. *Red Power: The American Indians' Fight for Freedom*. Lincoln, Neb.: University of Nebraska Press, 1999.

Kirk, Ruth. *Tradition & Change on the Northwest Coast: The Makah, Nuu-chah-nulth, Southern Kwakiutl, and Nuxalk*. Seattle, Wash.: University of Washington Press, 1986.

LaDuke, Winona. *All Our Relations: Native American Struggles for Land and Life*. Cambridge, Mass.: South End Press, 1999.

La Flesche, Francis. *The Osage and the Invisible World*. Garrick A. Bailey, ed. Norman, Okla.: University of Oklahoma Press, 1995.

Lame Deer, Archie Fire, and Richard Erdoes. *Gift of Power: The Life and Teachings of a Lakota Medicine Man*. Rochester, Vt: Bear & Company, 1992.

Matthiessen, Peter. *In the Spirit of Crazy Horse*. New York: Viking Penguin, 1991.

McIlwraith, T. F. *The Bella Coola Indians*. Toronto: University of Toronto Press, 1992; reprint of 1948 edition.

Means, Russell, with Marvin J. Wolf. *Where White Men Fear to Tread*. New York: St. Martin's Griffin, 1995.

Peltier, Leonard. *Prison Writings: My Life Is My Sun Dance*. New York: St. Martin's Griffin, 1999.

Philp, Kenneth R., ed. *Indian Self-Rule: First-Hand Accounts of Indian-White Relations from Roosevelt to Reagan*. Logan, Utah: Utah State University Press, 1995.

Steltenkamp, Michael F. *Black Elk: Holy Man of the Oglala*. Norman, Okla.: University of Oklahoma Press, 1993.

Walker, James R. *Lakota Belief and Ritual*. Lincoln, Neb.: University of Nebraska Press, 1991; reprint of 1980 edition.

PICTURE SOURCES

The pictures are reproduced courtesy of the following institutions and individuals. We gratefully acknowledge the assistance of staff at all the organizations who have supplied pictures, with special thanks to the photographer Ilka Hartmann for help and support.

American Antiquarian Society: 46; Ashmolean Museum, Oxford: 11 (BWP8X10); British Museum: xvi copyright © The British Museum; Colorado Historical Society, Stephen H. Hart Library: 99 (F154); Dane Coolidge and Mary Roberts Coolidge, *The Last of the Seris* New York: E. P. Dutton, 1939: xiii; De Bry, Theodore, *A Briefe and True Report of the New Found Land of Virginia,* 1590: 9; Drake, Samuel G., *Biography and History of the Indians of North America,* Boston: Benjamin B. Mussey, 1851: 14, 29; Fletcher, Alice C. and Francis La Flesche, *The Omaha Tribe (27th Annual Report of the Bureau of American Ethnology)* Washington: Government Printing Office, 1911: 119, 120, 121; Guildhall Library, Corporation of London: title page, opposite foreword, viii, xi, 93, 109, 124; Ilka Hartmann: 75, 112, 122, 129, 132, 135, 136, 139, all images copyright © Ilka Hartmann 2006; Phoebe Apperson Hearst Museum of Anthropology and the Regents of the University of California: 64 (15-5815); Library of Congress: xii (USZ262-101153), 4 (USZ262-99799), 7 (USZ262-49436), 12 (USZ262-8962), 20 (USZ262-2315), 29 (USZ62-10173), 58 (USZ262-111280), 60 (USZ2262-101260), 63 (USZ262-116525), 70 (USZ262-45902), 73 (USZ262-45903), 76 (USZ262-101284), 87 (USZ262-104562), 102 (USZ262-104561), 105 (USZ262-46972); Library of Virginia: 37; Magnus, Olavus, *A Description of the Northern Peoples,* 1555: 2; Marquette University, Raynor Memorial Libraries: 116 (00657); McKenney, Thomas L. and James Hall *History of the Indian Tribes of North America,* Philadelphia, 1835–36: 17, 21, 22, 23, 32, 41, 43, 45, 52, 55, 96; Mooney, James, *The Ghost-Dance Religion, with a Sketch of the Sioux Outbreak of 1890 (14th Annual Report of the Bureau of American Ethnology)* Washington: Government Printing Office, 1896: xv, 69; Mooney, James, *Myths of the Cherokee (19th Annual Report of the Bureau of American Ethnology)* Washington: Government Printing Office, 1900: 56; Mooney, James, *Calendar History of the Kiowa Indians (17th Annual Report of the Bureau of American Ethnology)* Washington: Government Printing Office, 1901: 92; National Galleries of Scotland: 18 (PEP HA 420); Naylor, Maria, *Authentic Indian Designs,* New York: Dover Publications, 1975: contents page, 15, 48, 131; Smithsonian Institution, National Anthropological Archives: endpapers (74-11816), 39 (44352), 50 (1034-A-1), 60 (893), 65 (3054-A), 80 (2987-B-12), 89 (72-8411), 95 (43,631), 97 (456), 101 (3678), 102 (43,201A), 107 (1659-A-1), 111 (86-4134), 114 (2517-A); Sugden, John, *Tecumseh* New York: Henry Holt, 1998; 31; Tulane University Library, New Orleans, La. Coll.: 25.

INDEX